ESTATE PUBLI

LEICESTERSHIRE
& RUTLAND

CW00328058

Street maps with index
Administrative Districts
Population Gazetteer
Road Map with index

COUNTY RED BOOKS

This atlas is intended for those requiring street maps of the historical and commercial centres of towns within the county. Each locality is normally presented on one or two pages and although, with many small towns, this space is sufficient to portray the whole urban area, the maps of large towns and cities are for centres only and are not intended to be comprehensive. Such coverage in Super and Local Red Books (see page 2).

Every effort has been made to verify the accuracy of information in this book but the publishers cannot accept responsibility for expense or loss caused by any error or omission. Information that will be of assistance to the user of these maps will be welcomed.

The representation of a road, track or footpath on the maps in this atlas is no evidence of the existence of a right of way

Street plans prepared and published by ESTATE PUBLICATIONS, Bridewell House, TENTERDEN, KENT, and based upon the ORDNANCE SURVEY mapping with the permission of The Controller of H. M. Stationery Office.

The Publishers acknowledge the co-operation of the local authorities of towns represented in this atlas.

COUNTY RED BOOK

LEICESTERSHIRE

& RUTLAND

contains street maps for each town centre

SUPER & LOCAL RED BOOKS

are street atlases with comprehensive local coverage

LEICESTER, LOUGHBOROUGH

including: Anstey, Blaby, Evington, Groby, Humberstone, Narborough, Oadby, Sileby, Syston, Wigston

CONTENTS

LEGEND TO STREET PLANS			
One-way street	→	Post Office	●
Pedestrianized	▨	Public Convenience	⊙
Car Park	🅿	Place of Worship	✚

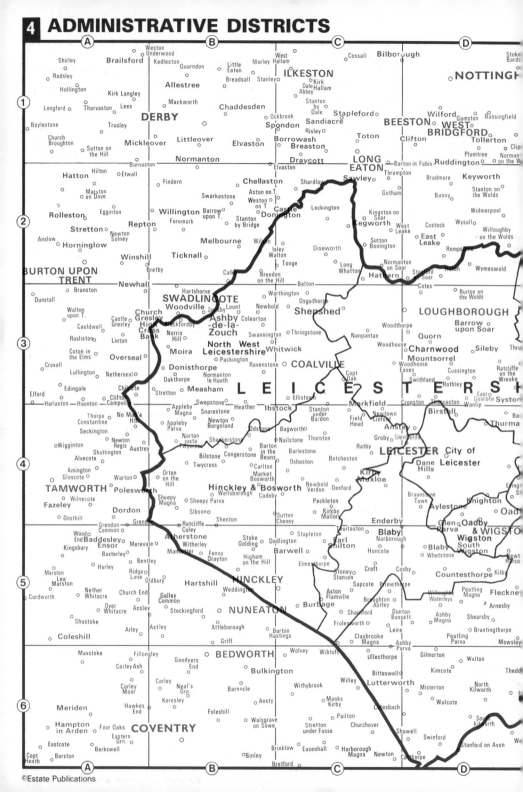

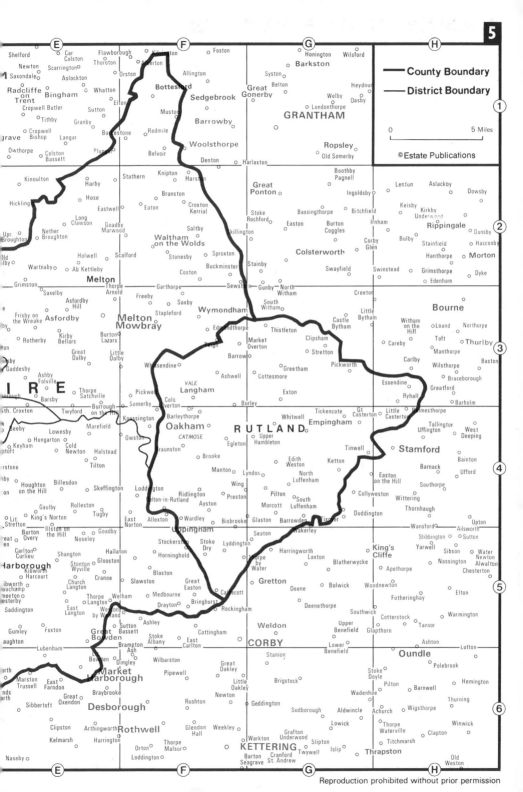

GAZETTEER INDEX TO ROAD MAP
with Populations

County of Leicestershire population 836,032
County of Rutland population 31,489

LEICESTERSHIRE Districts:

Blaby	82,700
Charnwood	141,806
Harborough	67,607
Hinckley & Bosworth	96,201
Leicester	270,493
Melton	45,112
North West Leicestershire	80,566
Oadby & Wigston	51,547

Place	Population	Ref
Ab Kettleby	544	9 E2
Allexton	38	9 F4
Anstey	6,192	8 C4
Appleby Magna	971	8 B4
Appleby Parva		8 B4
Arnesby	317	8 D5
Asfordby	3,086	9 E3
Asfordby Hill		9 E3
Ashby Folville		9 E3
Ashby Magna	290	8 D5
Ashby Parva	219	8 C5
Ashby Woulds	2,813	*
Ashby-de-la-Zouch	12,083	8 B3
Ashwell	237	9 F3
Aston Flamville	159	8 C5
Aylestone		8 D4
Ayston	38	9 F4
Bagworth	1,715	8 C4
Bardon	28	*
Barkby	337	8 D4
Barkby Thorpe	46	*
Barkestone		9 F2
Barlestone	2,288	8 C4
Barleythorpe	153	9 F4
Barrow	60	9 F3
Barrow upon Soar	4,773	8 D3
Barrowden	436	9 G4
Barsby		9 E3
Barton in the Beans		8 B4
Barwell		8 C5
Beaumont Chase	3	*
Beeby	81	9 E4
Belmisthorpe		9 H4
Belton	780	8 C3
Belton-in-Rutland	309	9 F4
Belvoir	281	9 F2
Billesdon	679	9 E4
Bilstone		8 B4
Birstall	11,770	8 D4
Bisbrooke	192	9 F4
Bittesby	12	*
Bitteswell	354	8 C6
Blaby	6,538	8 D5
Blaston	49	9 F5
Bottesford	2,981	9 F1
Branston		9 F2
Braunston	344	9 F4
Braunstone	12,945	8 D4
Breedon on the Hill	863	8 B2
Bringhurst	45	9 F5
Brooke	47	9 F4
Broughton and Old Dalby	1,336	9 E2
Broughton Astley	6,487	8 C5
Bruntingthorpe	389	8 D5
Buckminster	383	9 F2
Burbage	14,420	8 C5
Burley	286	9 F3
Burrough on the Hill		9 E4
Burton & Dalby	863	*
Burton Lazars		9 E3
Burton on the Wolds	940	8 D3
Burton Overy	259	9 E5
Butcheston		8 C4
Cadeby	161	8 B4
Caldecott	250	9 F5
Carlton	256	8 B4
Carlton Curlieu	42	9 E5
Castle Donington	6,313	8 C2
Catthorpe	179	*
Charley	208	*
Chilcote	94	8 B3
Church Langton		9 E5
Claybrooke Magna	502	8 C5
Claybrooke Parva	220	*
Clipsham	91	9 G3
Coalville	31,126	8 C3
Cold Newton	59	9 E4
Cold Overton and Knossington	333	9 F4
Coleorton	851	8 B3
Congerstone		8 B4
Copt Oak		8 C3
Cosby	3,390	8 D5
Cossington	488	*
Coston		9 F2
Cotes	41	8 D3
Cotesbach	195	8 C6
Cottesmore	2,487	9 G3
Countesthorpe	6,161	8 D5
Cranoe	32	9 E5
Croft	1,629	8 C5
Cropston and Thurcaston	2,012	8 D3
Croxton Kerrial	463	9 F2
Cussington		8 D3
Dadlington		8 C5
Dalby and Burton	863	*
Dane Hills		8 D4
Desford	3,565	8 C4
Diseworth		8 C2
Donisthorpe and Oakthorpe	2,041	8 B3
Drayton	147	9 F5
Dunton Bassett	777	8 D5
Earl Shilton		8 C5
East Goscote	3,038	8 D3
East Langton	344	9 E5
East Norton	97	9 F4
Eastwell		9 E2
Eaton	563	9 F2
Edith Weston	1,262	9 G4
Edmondthorpe		9 F3
Egleton	71	9 F4
Ellistown		8 C3
Elmesthorpe	508	8 C5
Empingham	824	9 G4
Enderby	5,767	8 C4
Essendine	210	9 H3
Evington		8 D4
Exton	557	9 G3
Fenny Drayton		8 B5
Field Head		8 C4
Fleckney	4,295	8 D5
Foxton	463	9 E5
Freeby	267	9 F3
Frisby	20	*
Frisby on the Wreake and Kirby	855	9 E3
Frolesworth	206	8 C5
Gaddesby	699	9 E3
Garthorpe	93	9 F3
Gaulby	88	9 E4
Gilmorton	859	8 D6
Glaston	156	9 G4
Glenfields	9,335	8 C4
Glen Parva	5,365	8 D4
Glooston	45	9 E5
Goadby	43	9 E5
Goadby Marwood		9 F2
Great Bowden		9 E5
Great Casterton	585	9 G4
Great Dalby		9 E3
Great Easton	538	9 F5
Great Glen	3,071	9 E5
Greetham	580	9 G3
Grimston	291	9 E2
Groby	7,321	8 C4
Gumley	118	9 E5
Gunthorpe	28	*
Hallaton	511	9 F5
Halstead		9 E4
Hambleton	128	*
Harby, Hose and Clawson	2,148	9 E2
Harston		9 F2
Hathern	1,791	8 C2
Heather	928	8 B4
Higham on the Hill	715	8 B5
Hinckley	58,537	8 B5
Hoby with Rotherby	531	9 E3
Holwell		9 E2
Horn	12	*
Horninghold	69	9 F5
Hose, Harby and Clawson	2,148	9 E2
Hoton	307	8 D2
Houghton on the Hill	1,681	9 E4
Humberstone		8 D4
Huncote	1,855	8 C5
Hungarton	239	9 E4
Husbands Bosworth	912	8 D6
Ibstock	5,493	8 B4
Illston on the Hill	181	9 E5
Isley cum Langley	78	*
Isley Walton		8 C2
Kegworth	3,405	8 C2
Ketton	1,708	9 G4
Keyham	147	9 E4
Kibworth Beauchamp	3,550	9 E5
Kibworth Harcourt	817	9 E5
Kilby	277	8 D5
Kimcote and Walton	526	8 D6
King's Norton	53	9 E4
Kirby Bellars and Frisby	855	9 E3
Kirby Muxloe	4,519	8 C4
Kirkby Mallory		8 C4
Knaptoft	40	*

Place	Ref	Place	Ref	Place	Ref
Knighton	8 D4	Packington 764	8 B3	Stoughton 217	8 D4
Knipton	9 F2	Peatling Magna 178	8 D5	Strathern 552	*
Knossington and		Peatling Parva 165	8 D5	Stretton 384	9 G3
Cold Overton 333	9 F4	Peckleton 985	8 C4	Stretton en le Field 36	8 B3
				Stretton Magna 12	*
Langham 1,095	9 F3	Pickwell	9 F3	Sutton Cheney 475	8 C4
Laughton 91	9 E5	Pickworth 216	9 G3	Swannington 1,195	8 B3
Launde 18	*	Pilton 19	9 G4	Swepstone 558	8 B4
Leicester 270,493	8 C4	Potters Marston 28	*	Swinford 496	8 D6
Leicester Forest East 4,921	*	Preston 175	9 F4	Swithland 212	8 D3
Leicester Forest West 43	*	Prestwold 82	*	Syston 10,900	8 D3
Leighfield 14	*	Primethorpe	8 C5		
Leire 571	8 C5			Teigh 43	9 F3
Little Bowden	9 E6	Queniborough 2,387	8 D3	Theddingworth 203	8 D6
Little Casterton 77	9 H4	Quorn 4,614	8 D3	Thistleton 108	9 G3
Little Dalby	9 E3			Thornton	8 C4
Little Stretton 61	9 E4	Ragdale	9 E3	Thorpe Arnold	9 E3
Lockington-Hemington 452	8 C2	Ratby 3,601	8 C4	Thorpe by Water 41	9 G5
Loddington 62	9 F4	Ratcliffe Culey	8 B5	Thorpe Langton 136	9 E5
Long Clawson, Hose and		Ratcliffe on the Wreake 133	8 D3	Thorpe Satchville	9 E3
Harby 2,148	9 E2	Ravenstone with		Thringstone	8 C3
Long Whatton 1,574	8 C2	Snibstone 1,874	8 B3	Thrussington 512	8 D3
Loughborough 48,664	8 D3	Rearsby 874	9 E3	Thurcaston and	
Lount	8 B3	Redmile 697	9 F2	Cropston 2,012	8 D3
Lowesby 85	9 E4	Ridlington 174	9 F4	Thurlaston 652	8 C5
Lubbesthorpe 77	*	Rolleston 43	9 E4	Thurmaston 9,146	8 D4
Lubenham 1,150	9 E6	Rotherby with Hoby 531	9 E3	Thurnby 2,838	8 D4
Lutterworth 7,380	8 C6	Rothley 3,141	8 D3	Tickencote 54	9 G4
Lyddington 396	9 F5	Ryhall 1,661	9 H3	Tilton 508	9 E4
Lyndon 85	9 G4			Tinwell 5	9 G4
		Saddington 225	9 E5	Tixover 103	9 G4
Manton 352	9 F4	Saltby	9 F2	Tonge	8 C2
Marefield 19	9 E4	Sapcote 2,628	8 C5	Tugby and Keythorpe 281	9 E4
Market Bosworth 2,019	8 B4	Saxby	9 F3	Tur Langton 166	*
Market Harborough 16,563	9 E6	Saxelby	9 E3	Twycross 739	8 B4
Market Overton 450	9 F3	Scalford 608	9 E2	Twyford & Thorpe 577	9 E4
Markfield 4,053	8 C3	Scraptoft 1,148	8 D4		
Measham 4,044	8 B3	Seagrave 426	*	Ullesthorpe 864	8 C6
Medbourne 405	9 F5	Seaton 178	9 G5	Ulverscroft 91	*
Melton Mowbray 24,312	9 E3	Sewstern	9 F3	Upper Hambleton	9 G4
Misterton 436	8 D6	Shackerstone 679	8 B4	Uppingham 3,140	9 F5
Moira	8 B3	Shangton 101	9 E5		
Morcott 345	9 G4	Sharnford 1,111	8 C5	Walcote	8 D6
Mountsorrel 6,033	8 D3	Shawell 151	8 D6	Waltham on the Wolds 798	9 F2
Mowsley 223	8 D5	Shearsby 205	8 D5	Walton on the Wolds 253	*
Muston	9 F2	Sheepy Magna with		Walton and Kimcote 526	8 D6
		Sheepy Parva 1,136	8 B4	Wanlip 181	8 D3
Nailstone 547	8 C4	Shenton	8 B4	Wardley 28	9 F4
Nanpantan	8 C3	Shepshed 12,961	8 C3	Wartnaby	9 E2
Narborough 7,613	8 C5	Sibson	8 B4	Welham 30	9 E5
Nevill Holt 44	*	Sileby 6,702	8 D3	Wellsborough	8 B4
Newbold	8 B3	Skeffington 178	9 E4	West Langton 51	*
Newbold Verdon 3,426	8 C4	Slawston 111	9 F5	Westrill and Starmore 12	*
Newton Burgoland	8 B4	Smeeton Westerby 346	9 E5	Whatborough 13	*
Newton Harcourt	8 D5	Smisby	8 B3	Whetstone 4,032	8 D5
Newtown Linford 971	8 C4	Snarestone 265	8 B4	Whissendine 1,177	9 F3
Normanton 28	*	Somerby 768	9 F3	Whitwell 37	9 G4
Normanton le Heath 114	8 B3	South Croxton 226	9 E4	Whitwick	8 B3
North Kilworth 537	8 D6	South Kilworth 386	8 D6	Wigston 35,439	8 D5
North Luffenham 548	9 G4	South Luffenham 458	9 G4	Wigston Parva 34	*
Norton juxta Twycross	8 B4	South Wigston	8 D5	Willoughby Waterleys 223	8 D5
Noseley 38	9 E5	Sproxton 459	9 F2	Wilson	8 C2
		Stanton under Bardon 604	8 C4	Wing 312	9 F4
Oadby 19,579	8 D4	Stapleford	9 F3	Wistow 249	*
Oakham 8,691	9 F4	Stapleton	8 C5	Withcote 36	*
Oakthorpe and		Stathern 552	9 E2	Witherley 1,513	8 B5
Donisthorpe 2,041	8 B3	Staunton Harold 116	*	Woodhouse 2,215	8 D3
Odstone	8 B4	Stockerston 33	9 F5	Woodhouse Eaves	8 C3
Old Dalby and		Stoke Dry 37	9 F5	Woodthorpe	8 C3
Broughton 1,336	9 E2	Stoke Golding 1,607	8 B5	Worthington 1,406	8 B3
Orton on the Hill	8 B4	Stonesby	9 F2	Wymeswold 1,063	8 D2
Osbaston 259	8 C4	Stoney Stanton 3,113	8 C5	Wymondham 588	9 F3
Osgathorpe 369	8 C3	Stonton Wyville 27	9 E5		
Owston and Newbold 88	9 F4				

Population figures are based upon the 1991 census and relate to the local authority area or parish as constituted at that date Boundaries of the districts are shown on pages 4-5. Places with no population figure form part of a larger local authority area or parish.

Population figures in bold type.

*Place not included on map due to limitation of space

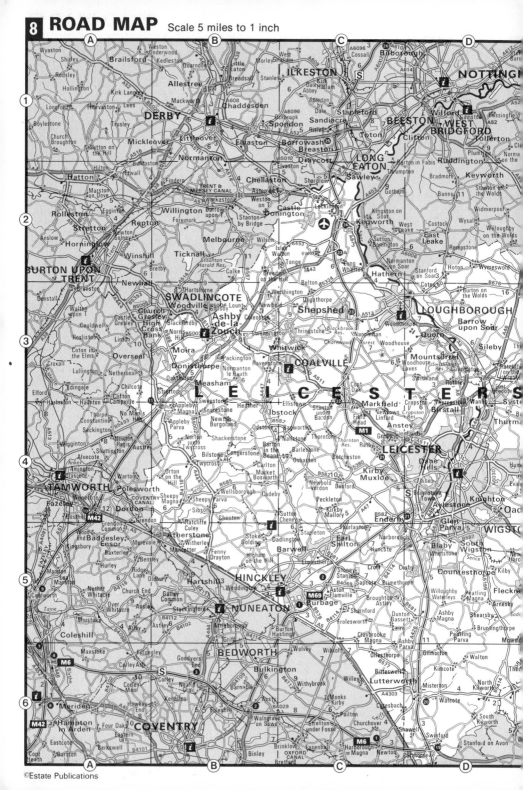

ROAD MAP

8 Scale 5 miles to 1 inch

©Estate Publications

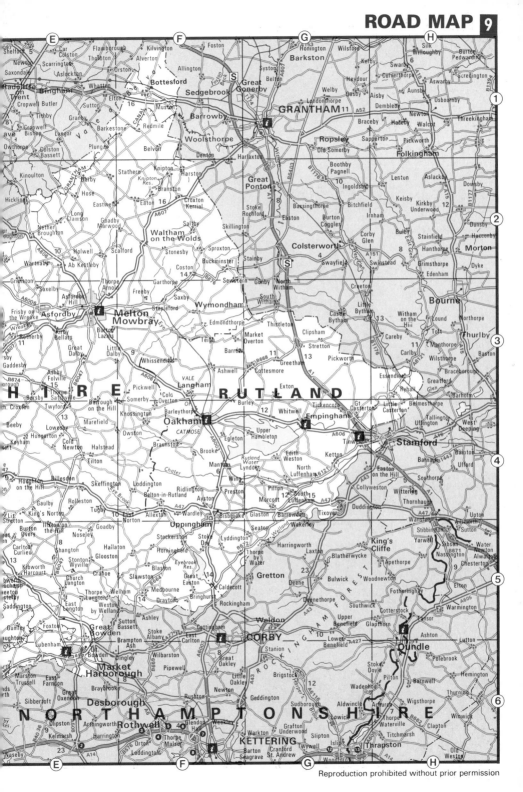

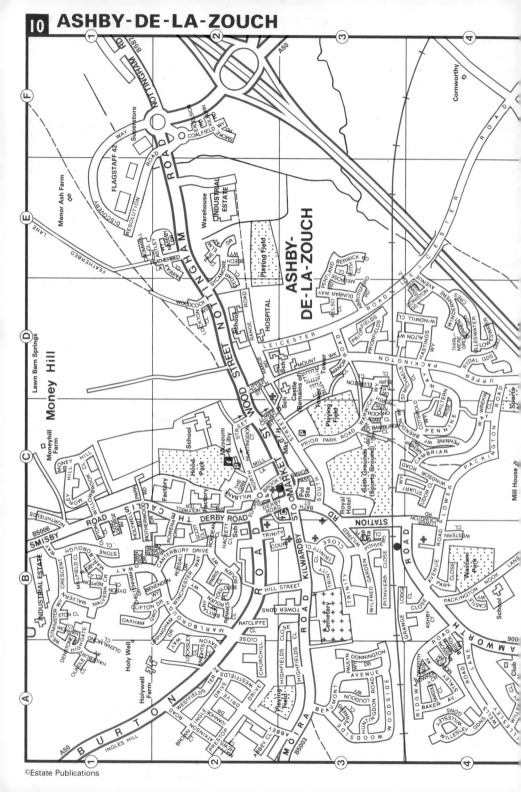

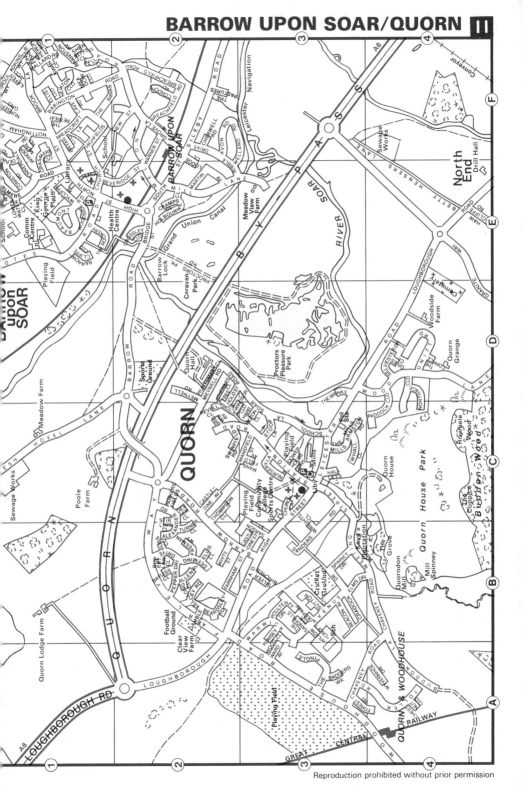

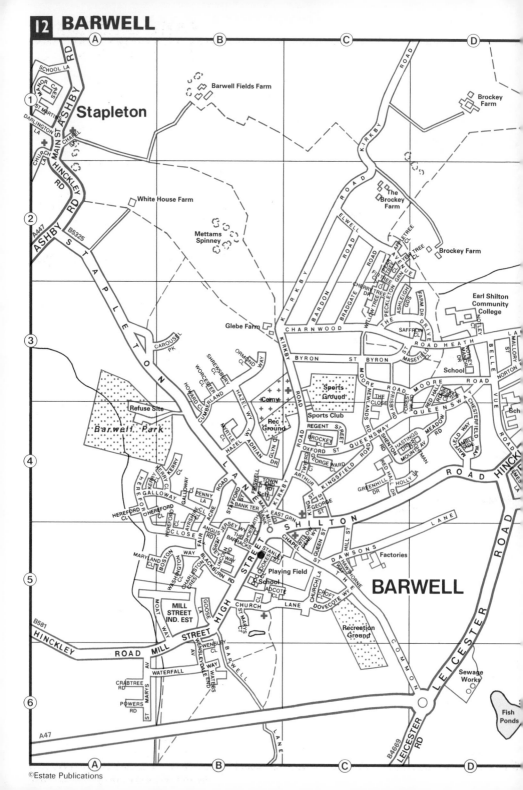

Stapleton

BARWELL

Barwell Fields Farm

Brockey Farm

The Brockey Farm

Brockey Farm

White House Farm

Mettams Spinney

Earl Shilton Community College

Glebe Farm

School

Sports Ground

Sports Club

Rec Ground

Cemy

Carousel Pk

Refuse Site

Barwell Park

Town Hd Sch

School

Playing Field

Factories

Recreation Ground

Mill Street Ind. Est

Sewage Works

Fish Ponds

SCHOOL LA
MANOR CRES
ST MARTINS
DARLINGTON LA
CHURCH LA
MAIN ST
CHAPEL
HINCKLEY RD
ASHBY RD
A447
B5325
STAPLETON LANE
ASHBY RD

KIRKBY ROAD
ELWELL ROAD
BARDON ROAD
BRADGATE ROAD
ASH TREE
WILLOW TREE
PECKLETON CL
FIR TREE CL
THE TREES
CHERRY TREE DR
CHARNWOOD
SAFFRON
MOORE ROAD
BYRON ST
BYRON
HEATH
MASEFIELD
QUEENSWAY
FOREST WARD
THE CLOSE
NEWLANDS RD
SHENTON RD
HASTINGS RD
MEADOW
MOUNT AV
RED HILL
HOLLY LA
GREENHILL DR
KINGSFIELD RD
ARTHUR ST
FORGE WARD
OXFORD ST
REGENT STREET
BROCKEY CL
GLYN DR
ADRIAN
HAZEL WY
HAZEL WY
MYRTLE CL
HOWARD CL
CUMBERLAND CL
WORCESTER CL
SHREWSBURY CL
ORMOND CL
KIRKBY WAY
LANE
ACRE ROAD
STAFFORD CL
FINSWELL CL
BANK TER
KING ST
ST GEORGE ST
QUEEN ST
DAWSONS
HAWTHORNE
CHURCH LA
DOVECOTE WY
HILL LA
LANE
CROFT
SHILTON STREET
CHAPEL
EAST GRN
THE SPINN
BARRACKS
ANGUS RD
JERSEY WY
LINCOLN WY
FAIR
AYRSHIRE CL
HEREFORD CLOSE
PENNY LA
KERRY CL
GALLOWAY
KERRY CL
HEREFORD CL
GALLOWAY
MARY CL
LANDSTON CL
BOSTON WAY
WASHINGTON
CHARLESTON RD
BLACKBURN RD
ADCOTE
MOAT WAY
MILL STREET
GOOSE
ST MARYS
CHURCH LA
WENSLEYDALE CL
WENSLEYDALE END
WATERFALL
WATERS END
CRABTREE RD
POWERS RD
ST MARYS AV
HINCKLEY ROAD
B581
MILL STREET
BARWELL
HIGH STREET
A47

KIRKBY ROAD
MALLORY
NORTON
BELLE VUE ROAD
MANOR DR
CHESTERFIELD WAY
MAYFIELD WAY
AMBLESIDE
HINCKLEY ROAD
WESTFIELD
Sch

LEICESTER ROAD
COMMON
B4669 LEICESTER RD
LANE

©Estate Publications

EARL SHILTON

13

EARL SHILTON

Elmesthorpe

ELMESTHORPE ESTATE
(Land Settlement Association)

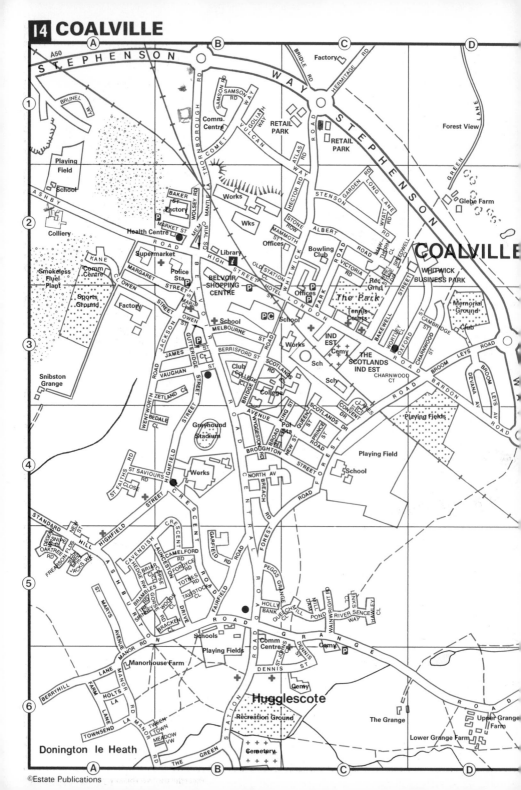

14 COALVILLE

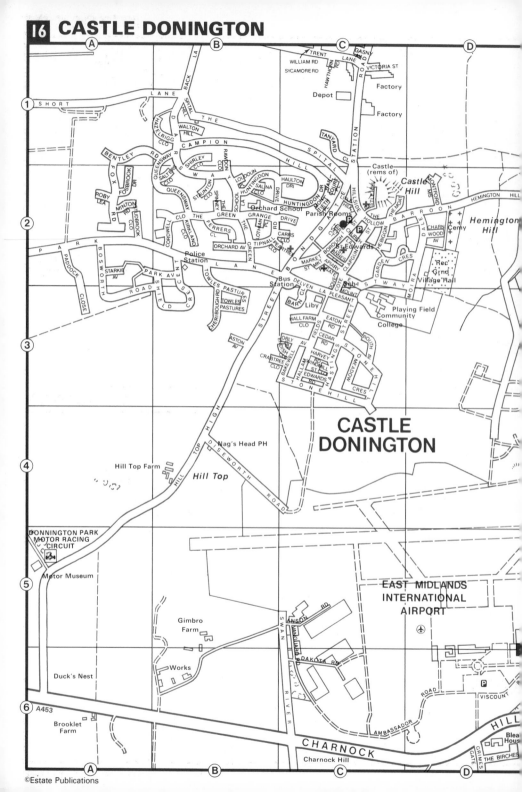

A   B   C   D

SHORT

BACK LANE

WILLIAM RD
SYCAMORE RD
TRENT LANE
GASNY
VICTORIA ST
Factory
Factory
Depot

THE SPITAL LANE

HAZELRIGG CLO
ELRIGG CLO
WALTON HILL
SPITAL
CAMPION
TANYARD
STATION RD
SPITAL CLO
STATION

BENTLEY RD
FOX
QUEENSWAY
SALTERSGATE
SHIRLEY CLO
STAUNTON CLO
SPINNEY
RAWDON CLO
LOUDOUN PL
HUNTINGDON CLO
SALINA CLO
HUNTINGDON DRIVE
HAULTON DRI
HUNTINGDON DRI
Castle (rems of)
Castle Hill
HEMINGTON HILL
MONTFORT CLO

ROBY LEA
FOXCROFT
LUDBROOK
MINTON CLO
QUEENSWAY
CORDWELL CLO
THE GREEN
KIRKLAND CLO
TOOKS
THE FERRERS CL
THE GREEN
GRANGE DRIVE
CARRS CLO
TIPNALL RD
PEARTREE
Orchard School
Parish Rooms
P
P
THE HOLLOW
THE MOAT
DALE
CHARN WOOD AV
BARROON
Hemington Hill
Cemy

PARK
PADDOCK CLOSE
BOSWORTH
STARKIE AV
PARK AV
SHIELD
ROAD
ORCHARD AV
Police Station
THE GREEN
TOWLES PASTURES
HERIBOUGH RD
TOWLES PASTURES
ASTON AV
LANE
HIGH STREET
DELVEN LA
Bus Station
MARKET ST
CLAPGUN ST
BOROUGH
St Edwards
APIARY
MOTE
Ash
MOUNT
Liby
MOUNT PLEASANT
GARDEN ST
CRES
MOIRA ST
EASTWAY
Rec Grnd
Village Hall
Community College
Playing Field

BAR
HALL FARM CLO
ORLY AV
CRABTREE CLO
BAKEWELL CLO
HALLAM FIELDS RD
CEDAR RD
EATON CLO
WINDMILL ST
HARVEY RD
St Edwards
WINDMILL ST
CRES
ROUND HILL
STONEHILL
MEADOW
STONE HILL

HILL TOP
DISEWORTH ROAD
Nag's Head PH
Hill Top Farm
Hill Top

CASTLE DONINGTON

DONINGTON PARK MOTOR RACING CIRCUIT
Motor Museum

⑤ EAST MIDLANDS INTERNATIONAL AIRPORT

Gimbro Farm
SWAN
ANSON RD
MALLARD
DAKOTA RD
Works
Duck's Nest
RIVER
P
VISCOUNT
ROAD

⑥ A453
Brooklet Farm
AMBASSADOR
HILL
Blea Hous
GATE
GRIMES
THE BIRCHES
CHARNOCK
Charnock Hill

A   B   C   D

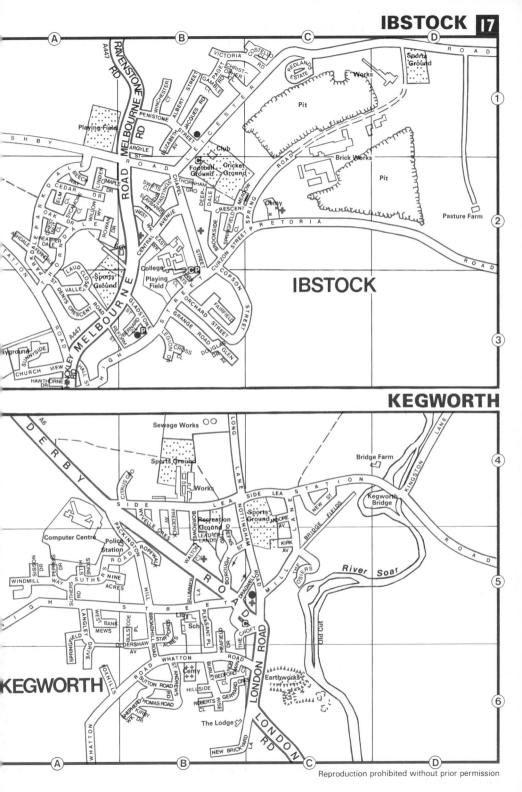

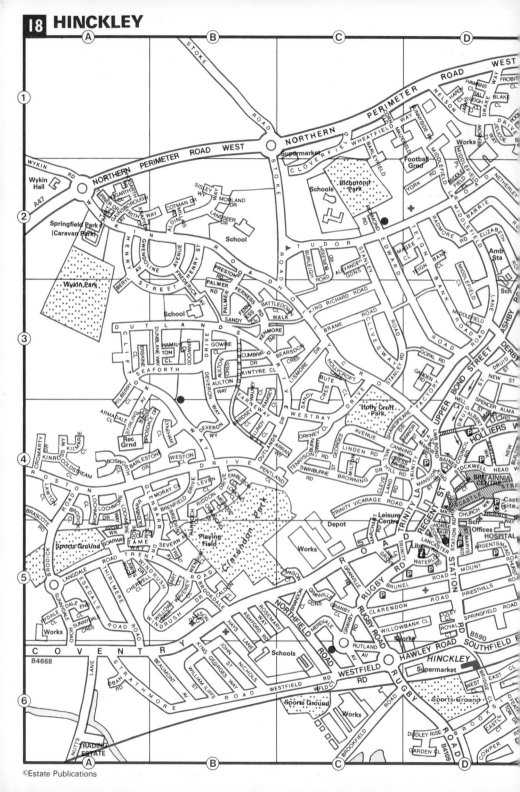

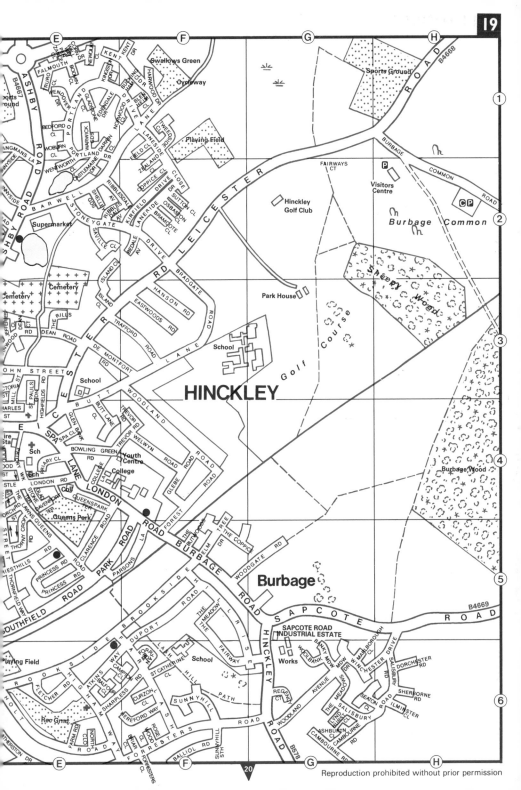

19

HINCKLEY

Burbage

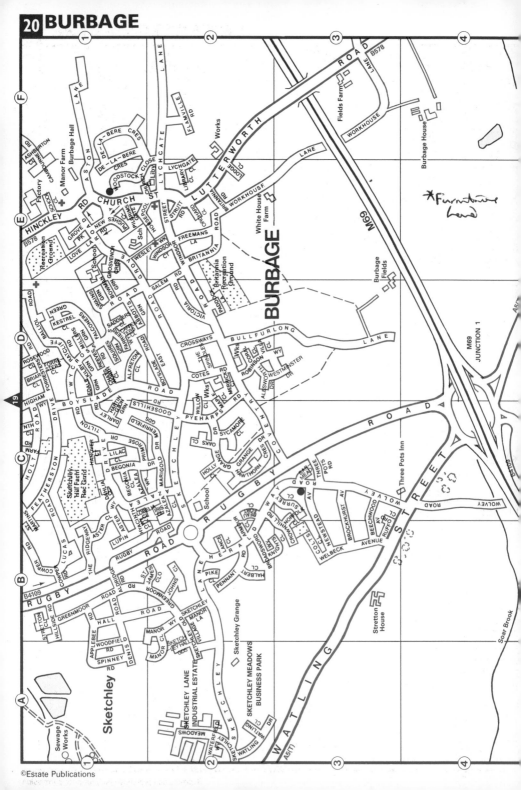

BURBAGE

Sketchley

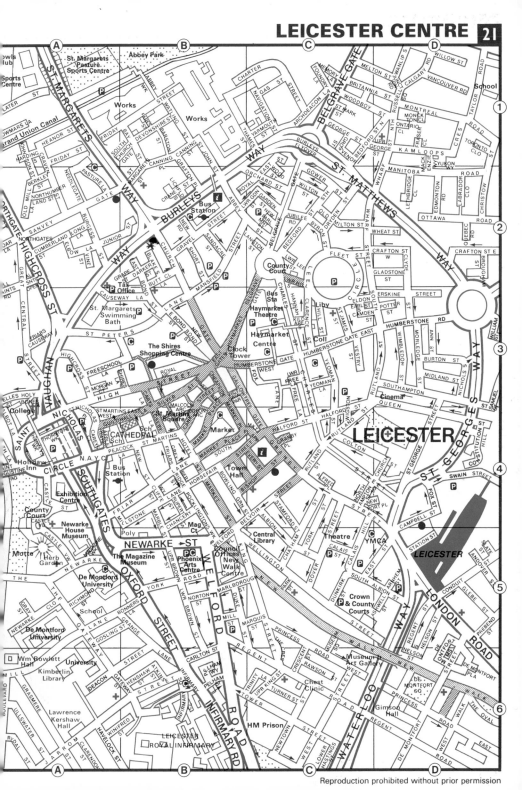

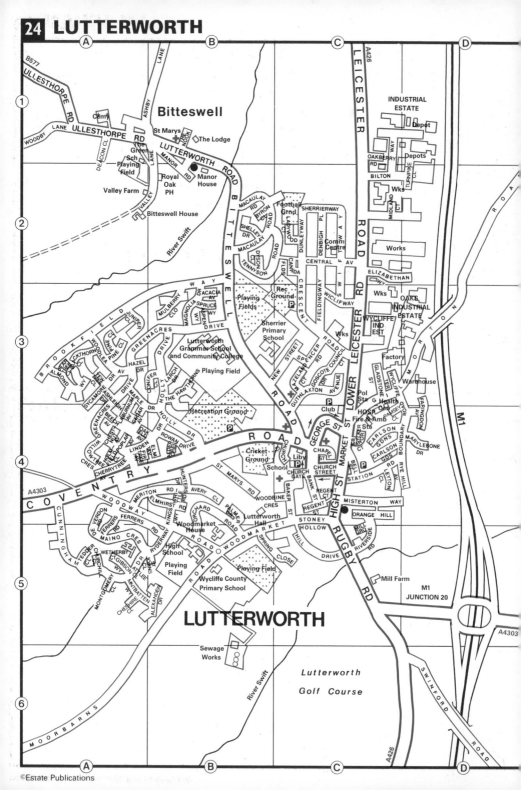

Bitteswell

LUTTERWORTH

Lutterworth Golf Course

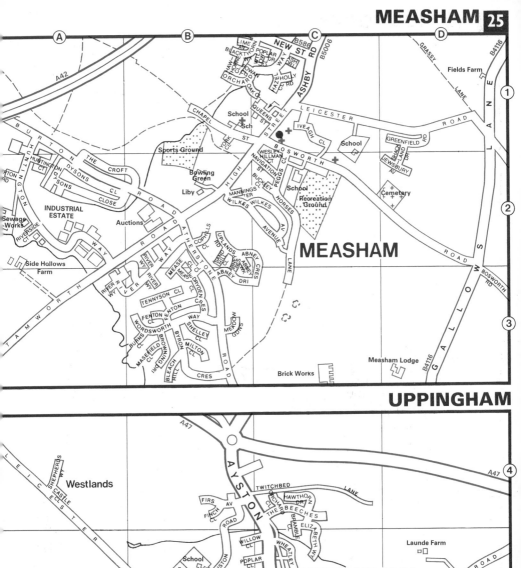

MEASHAM

UPPINGHAM

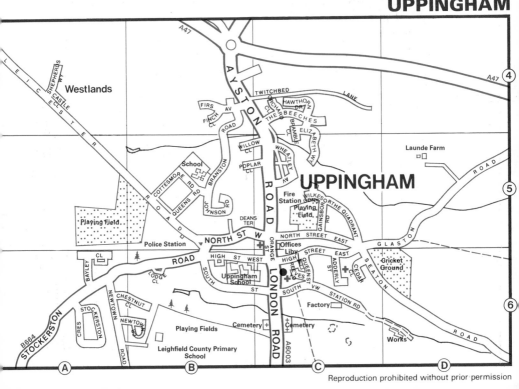

UPPINGHAM

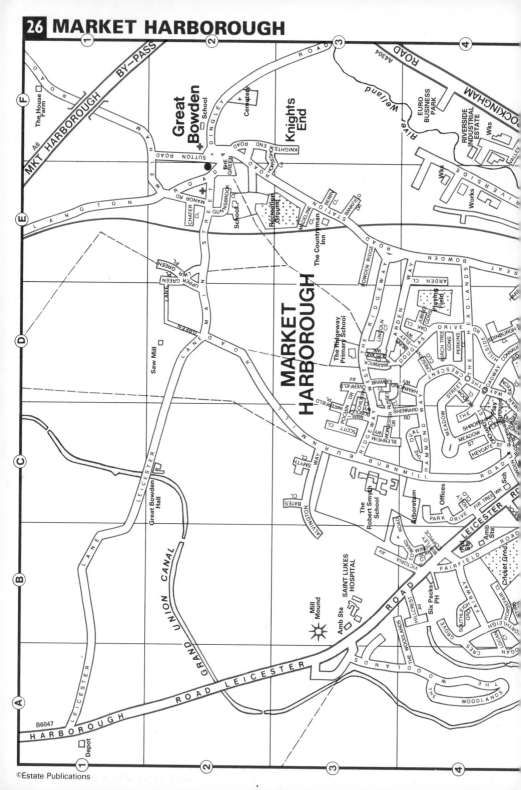

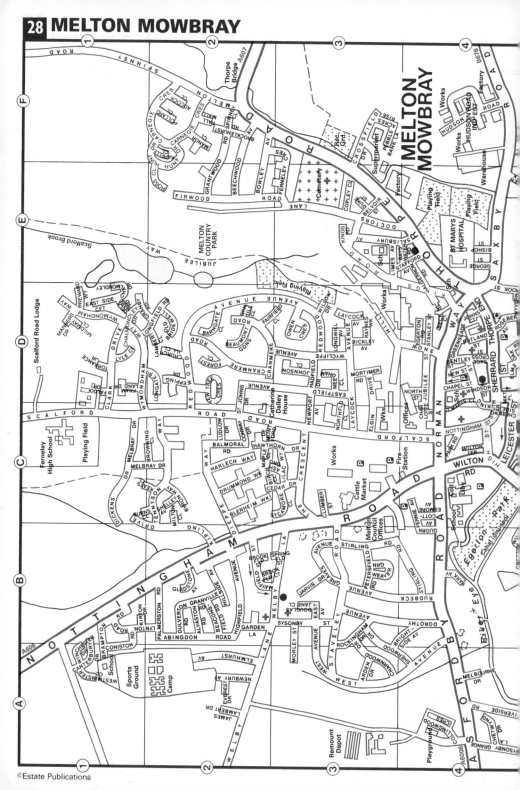

MELTON MOWBRAY

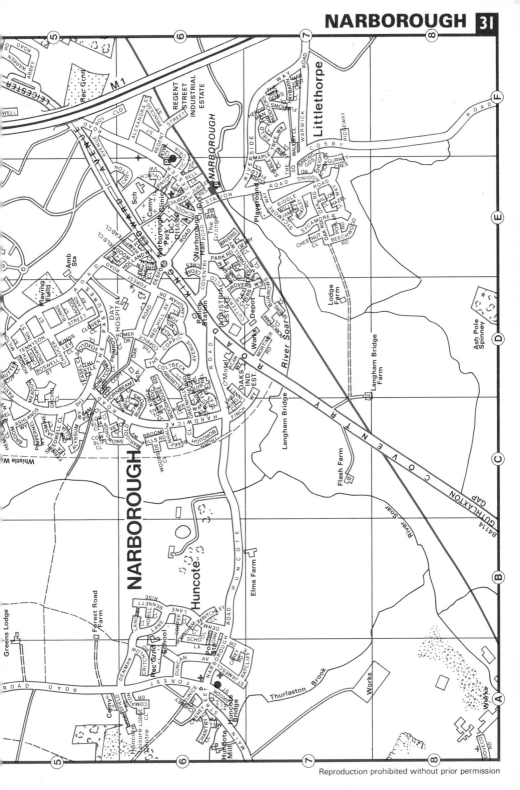

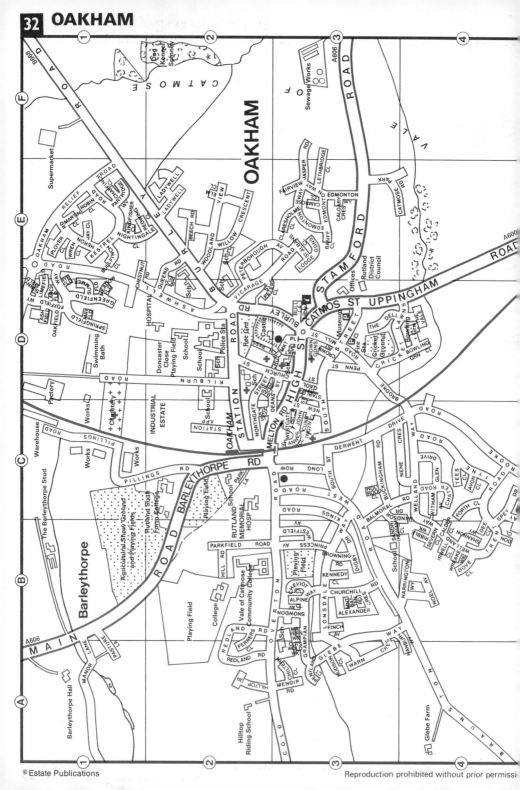

OAKHAM

CATMOSE

Barleythorpe

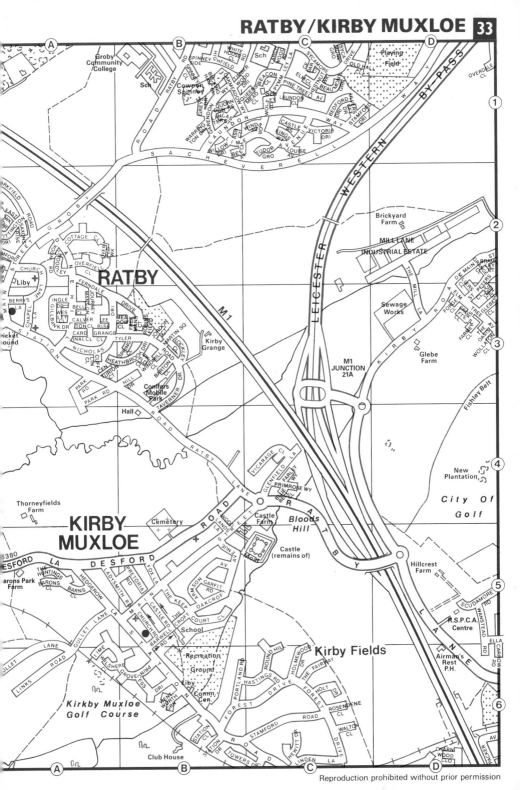

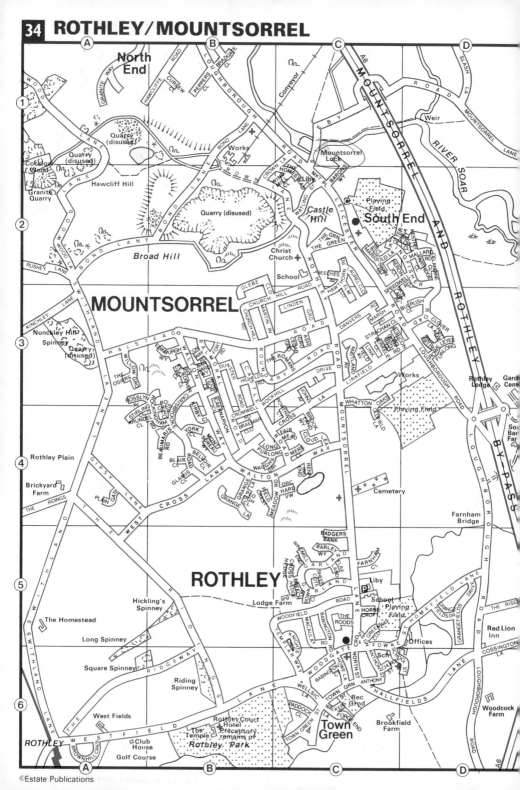

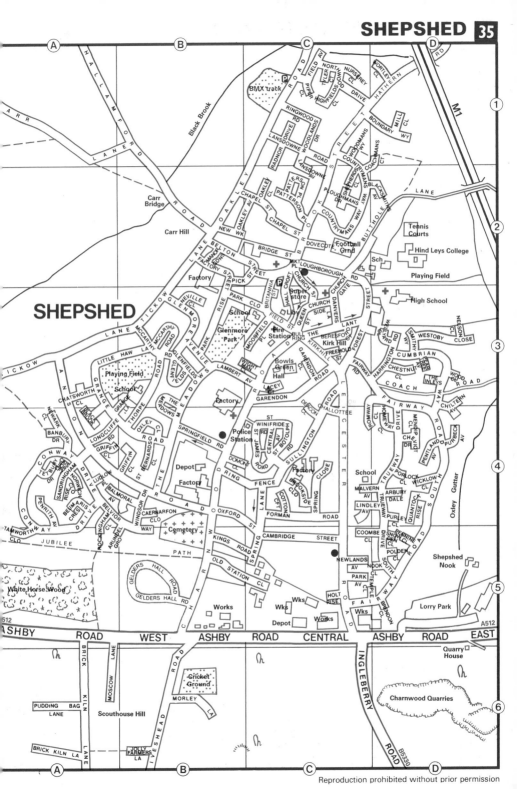

SHEPSHED

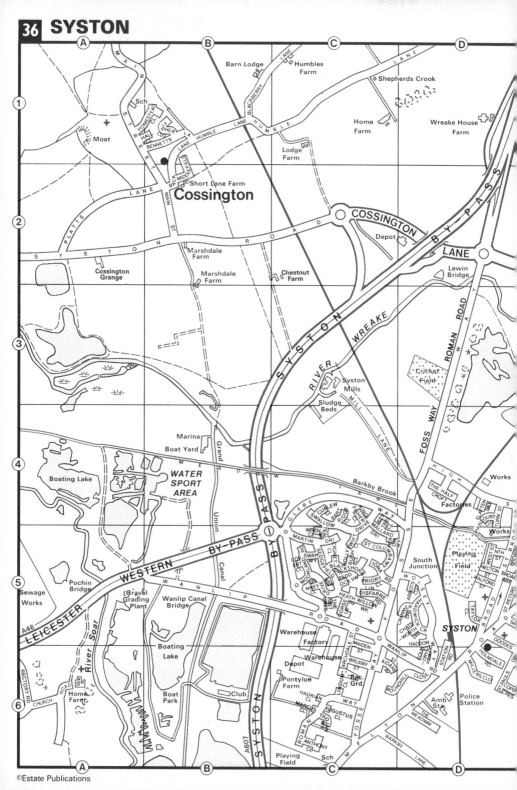

36 SYSTON

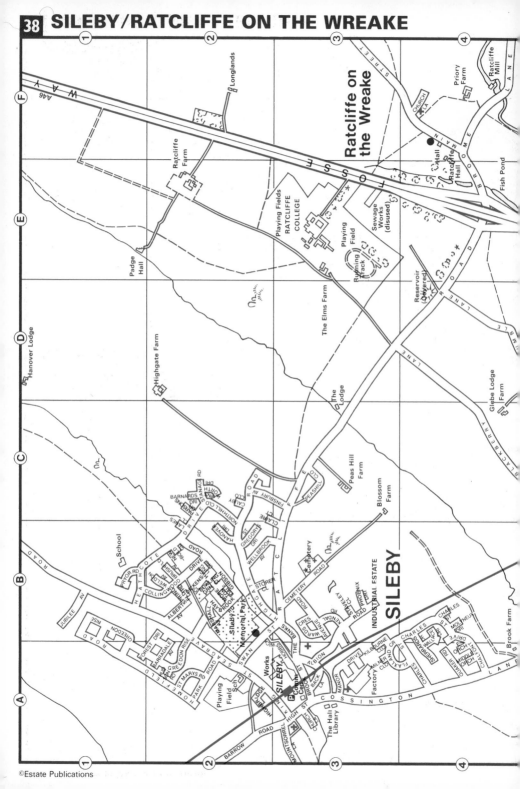

Ratcliffe on
the Wreake

SILEBY

©Estate Publications

A- Z INDEX TO STREETS

The Index includes some names for which there is insufficient space on the maps. These names are preceded by an * and are followed by the nearest adjoining thoroughfare.

eorge Foster Clo 13 G2
eorge Geary Clo 12 D2
eorge St 12 C4
eorge Ward Clo 12 C4
lyn Clo 12 B4
oose La 12 B5
reen La 13 F2
reenhill Dri 12 C4
arrison Clo 13 G2
astings Dri 12 C4
awthorne Way 12 C5
azel Way 12 B4
eath Ct 13 E4
eath La 12 D3
eath La Sth 13 E3
ereford Clo 12 A4
igh St, Barwell 12 B5
igh St, Earl Shilton 13 G3
igh Tor East 13 F2
igh Tor West 13 F2
ighfield St 13 E4
ill St 12 C5
ill Top 13 G2
inckley Rd, Barwell 12 A5
inckley Rd,
Earl Shilton 13 E4
inckley Rd, Stapleton 12 A2
olly La 12 C4
ollydene Cres 13 E3
oward Clo 12 B3
urst Rd 13 F4
NDUSTRIAL ESTATES:
Mill St Ind Est 12 B5
Oaks Ind Est 13 F3
Station Rd Ind Est 13 F3
ydene Clo 13 G3
ames St 13 F3
ersey Way 12 B5
eats Clo 13 G2
eats La 13 F2
erry Clo 12 B4
ing Richards Hill 13 H2
ing St 12 C4
ings Row 13 F3
ings Walk 13 F3
ingsfield Rd 12 C4
irkby Rd, Barwell 12 B4
irkby Rd, East Shilton 13 F1
nights Link 13 H2
aburnum Dri 13 E4
and Society La 13 F3
eicester Rd, Barwell 12 C6
eicester Rd,
Earl Shilton 13 G2
eighton Cres 13 G6
ime Gro 13 E4
incoln Rd 12 B5
ovelace Cres 13 G6
ucas Way 13 F4
yndene Clo 13 F3
ain St 12 A1
allory St 12 D3
alt Mill Bank 12 B4
anor Cres 12 A1
aple Way 13 E4
ary St 13 G2
aryland Clo 12 A5
asefield Clo 12 C3
ayfield Way 12 D4
eadow Court Rd 13 G3
eadow Rd 12 D4
elton St 13 E3
etcalfe St 13 F3
ill La 13 H2
ill St 12 B6
oat Way 12 B5
ona St 13 F4
ontgomery Rd 13 H3
oore Rd 12 C3
ount Av 12 C4
ountfield Rd 13 F3
yrtle Clo 12 B4
ew St 13 E3
ewlands Rd 12 C3
ock Verges 13 H2
orthleigh Way 13 G3
orton Rd 12 D3
otley Clo 12 D3
otley Manor Dri 12 D3
ursery Gdns 13 E4
akdale Rd 13 E4
aks Way 13 F3
rmond Clo 12 B3
xford St, Barwell 12 C4
xford St, East Shilton 13 G3
ark Clo 13 F2
ark Rd 13 F2
eartree Clo 12 C2
eckleton Grn 12 C3
Peggs Clo 13 G3
Penny La 12 B4
Powers Rd 12 A6
Prospect Way 13 F2
Queen St 12 C5
Queensway 12 C4
Red Hall Dri 12 C4
Red Hall Rd 12 D3
Regent St 12 C4
Roman Clo 13 H2
Ronald Toon Rd 13 H3
Rossendale Rd 13 E3
Saffron Clo 12 D3
St Martins 12 A1
St Marys Av 12 A6
St Marys Ct 12 B5
Sandringham Av 13 E4
School La 12 A1
Shenton Rd 12 C4
Shilton Rd 12 C5
Shoesmith Clo 12 B5
Shrewsbury Clo 12 B3
Spring Gdns 13 G2
Stafford St 12 B4
Stanley St 12 B5
Stapleton La 12 A2
Station Rd, Earl Shilton 13 F4
Station Rd,
Elmesthorpe 13 F5
Stoneycroft Rd 13 F4
The Barracks 12 B5
The Beeches 13 G2
The Cloisters 13 F3
The Close 12 C3
The Common 12 C5
The Crescent 13 E6
The Drive 12 C3
The Grange 13 F4
The Hollow 13 F3
The Leecroft 13 G3
The Poplars 13 H2
The Roundhills 13 G6
Thurlaston La 13 H2
Tom Eatough Ct 13 H3
Tower Rd 13 F2
Townend Rd 12 B4
Twyford Ct 12 C4
Ullswater Clo 13 G3
Vicarage Ct 13 G3
Vicarage St 13 G2
Washington Clo 12 B5
Waterfall Way 12 B6
Waters End 12 B6
Waughan St 13 G2
Weaver Rd 13 G3
Wensley Clo 12 B6
Wensleydale Av 12 B6
West St 13 G2
Wightman Rd 12 D4
Wilenins Clo 13 F4
Wilf Bown 13 H2
Wilkinson La 13 F5
Willow Tree Clo 12 C3
Willowdene Way 12 C5
Windermere Clo 13 F3
Wood St 13 F3
Worcester Clo 12 B3
Yew Tree Clo 12 C2

CASTLE DONINGTON

Ambassador Rd 16 C6
Anson Rd 16 C5
Apiary Gate 16 C2
Aston Av 16 B3
Back La 16 B1
Bakewell 16 C3
Barn Clo 16 C3
Barroon 16 C2
Bentley Rd 16 A1
Bondgate 16 C2
Borough St 16 C2
Bosworth Rd 16 A2
Campion Hill 16 B1
Carrs Clo 16 C2
Castle Hill 16 C2
Cavendish Clo 16 C3
Cedar Rd 16 C3
Charnock Hill 16 C6
Charnwood Av 16 D2
Cheriborough Rd 16 B3
Church La 16 C1
Clapgun St 16 C2
Cordwell Clo 16 B2
Crabtree Clo 16 B3
Dakota Rd 16 C6
Darsway 16 B1
Delven La 16 C2
Diseworth Rd 16 B4
Dove Cote 16 C2
Eastway 16 C2
Eaton Rd 16 C3
Ferrers Clo 16 B2
Fosbrook Dri 16 A2
Fox Rd 16 A2
Garden Cres 16 C2
Gasny Av 16 C1
Grange Dri 16 B2
Grimes Gate 16 D6
Hall Farm Clo 16 C3
Hallam Fields 16 C3
Harcourt Pl 16 C2
Harvey Ct 16 C2
Harvey Rd 16 C3
Hastings St 16 C3
Haulton Dri 16 C2
Hawthorn Rd 16 C1
Hazelrigg Clo 16 B1
Hemington Hill 16 D2
High St 16 B4
Hill Top 16 B4
Hillside 16 C2
Huntingdon Dri 16 B2
Kirkland Clo 16 B2
Little Hill 16 C2
Lothian Pl 16 B2
Loudoun Pl 16 B2
Market Pl 16 C2
Market St 16 C2
Meadow Cres 16 C3
Minton Rd 16 A2
Moira Dale 16 D2
Montford Mews 16 D2
Montieth Pl 16 C2
Mount Pleasant 16 C3
Orchard Av 16 B2
Orly Av 16 C3
Paddock Clo 16 A2
Park Av 16 B2
Park La 16 A2
Peartree Clo 16 B2
Queensway 16 B2
Rawdon Clo 16 B1
Roby Lea 16 A2
Routh Av 16 C3
St Annes La 16 C2
St Edwards Rd 16 C3
Salina Clo 16 B2
Salters Clo 16 B2
School La 16 B2
Shield Cres 16 B3
Shirley Clo 16 B1
Short La 16 A1
Spital Hill 16 B1
Starkie Av 16 A2
Station Rd 16 C1
Staunton Clo 16 B2
Stone Hill 16 C3
Studbrook Clo 16 A2
Swan River 16 C5
Sycamore Rd 16 C1
Tanyard Clo 16 C1
The Biggin 16 C2
The Birches 16 D6
The Green 16 B2
The Hollow 16 C2
The Moat 16 C2
The Spinney 16 B2
The Spital 16 B1
Tipnall Rd 16 B2
Towles Pastures 16 B3
Trent La 16 C1
Vanguard Rd 16 C5
Victoria St 16 C1
Viscount Rd 16 D6
Walton Hill 16 B1
William Rd 16 C1
Windmill Clo 16 C3

COALVILLE

Abbey Rd 15 H1
Abbotts Oak Dri 15 F2
Agar Nook La 15 H2
Albert Rd 14 C2
Ashburton Rd 14 A5
Ashby Rd 14 A2
Ashtree Rd 14 A5
Atlas Rd 14 C1
Avenue Rd 14 B4
Baker St 14 B2
Bakewell St 14 C3
Bardon Clo 15 F5
Bardon Rd 14 D3
Beacon Cres 15 G4
Bedale Clo 14 A4
Beech Rd 15 E4
Belgrave Clo 15 H2
Belton Clo 15 G2
Belvoir Rd 14 B2
Belvoir Shopping
Centre 14 B2
Berrisford St 14 B3
Berryhill La 14 A6
*Blackbrook Ct,
Bradgate Dri 15 G4
Blackbrook Dri 15 F4
Blackwood 15 F2
Botts Way 15 E4
Bracken Clo 14 B5
Bradgate Dri 15 G4
Brambles Rd 14 A5
Breach Rd 14 B4
Briar Clo 14 A5
Bridge Rd 14 B3
Bridle Rd 14 C1
Broad St 14 B4
Broom Leys Av 14 D3
Broom Leys Rd 14 D3
Broughton St 14 B4
Brunel Way 14 A1
Cambridge St 14 D3
Camelford Rd 14 B5
Castle Rock Dri 15 G1
Cavendish Cres 14 A5
Central Rd 14 B4
Charnborough Rd 15 G3
Charnwood Ct 14 C3
Charnwood St 14 D3
Chestnut Gro 15 F3
Clarke Rd 15 G3
College Clo 14 B3
Comet Way 14 B1
Convent Dri 14 C4
Copse Clo 14 B5
Crescent Rd 14 B4
Cromore Clo 15 G3
Cropston Dri 15 F4
Curlew Clo 15 E4
Dauphine Clo 15 H3
Degens Way 14 A5
Dennis St 14 B6
Devana Av 14 D3
Deveron Clo 15 H3
Dove Rd 15 E4
Drome Clo 15 H3
Dunbar Rd 15 G3
Durris Clo 15 H3
Fairfield Rd 14 B5
Farm La 14 A6
Fordyce Rd 14 B5
Forest Rd 14 B5
Frearson Fields 14 A5
Garden Rd 14 C2
Garendon Rd 15 G4
Garfield Rd 14 B5
Gillamore Dri 15 E1
Glen Way 15 E4
Goliath Way 14 B1
Gorse Rd 14 B5
Grange Rd 14 C5
Grasmere 15 G2
Green La 14 D2
Greenfields Dri 15 F2
Greenhill Rd 15 F3
Gutteridge St 14 B3
Hall Gate 15 G3
Hall La 15 E1
Hamilton Rd 15 G3
Haslyn Walk 15 F3
Hawley Clo 14 C5
Hawthorn Clo 14 C2
Hector Rd 14 C2
Hedge Row 14 A5
Helmsdale Clo 15 H3
Hermitage Rd 14 C1
Heron Way 15 E4
High St 14 B2
Highfield St 14 A5
Hilary Cres 15 E1
Holly Bank 14 B5
Holts La 14 A6
Hotel St 14 B3
INDUSTRIAL ESTATES:
The Scotlands Ind Est 14 C3
Whitwick Business
Park 14 D2
Jacks Walk 14 A5
Jackson St 14 B3
Jacque Mart Clo 15 H3
James St 14 B3
Kane Clo 14 A2
Kenmoor Cres 15 G3
King St 14 C4
Kingfisher Clo 15 F2
Kirkhill Clo 15 H3
Kirton Rd 15 H3
Lancaster Clo 15 H2
Launceston Dri 14 B5
Leicester Rd 15 G1
Linford Cres 15 F2
Links Clo 14 C5
London Rd 14 C3
Long La 14 C2
Longcliff Rd 15 G4
Mammoth St 14 C2
Manor Rd 14 A6
Mantle La 14 B2
Maplewell 15 F3
Margaret St 14 A2
Market St 14 B2
Marlborough Clo 14 B3
Meadow La 15 F2
Meadow View 14 A6
Melbourne St 14 B3
Memorial Sq 14 B2
Mickledon Grn 15 E1
Mill Dam 14 C5
Mill Pond 14 C5
Muscovy Rd 15 E4
Nelson Fields 15 F2
Nene Way 15 E4
Neville Dri 15 F2
New St, Coalville 14 C4
New St, Hugglescote 14 A5
North Av 14 B4
Northfields Dri 15 F3
Oak Clo 15 E4
Oakham Dri 15 G2
Oaktree Rd 14 A5
Old Station Clo 14 B2
Owen St 14 A2
Oxford St 14 C3
Park Rd 14 C3
Peggs Grange 14 B5
Peldar Pl 15 G3
Perran Av 15 E2
Peterfield Rd 15 E1
Prince St 14 C4
Queen St 14 C4
Quelch Clo 14 B5
Quorn Cres 15 F3
River Sence Way 14 C5
Robin Rd 15 E4
Rochdale Cres 15 H2
Romans Cres 15 H3
Rowan Av 15 F3
St Clares Ct 14 C4
St Davids Cres 15 G2
St Faiths Clo 14 A4
St Faiths Rd 14 A4
St Ives 15 F4
St Johns Clo 14 B6
St Marys Av 14 A5
St Saviours Rd 14 A4
Samson Rd 14 B1
Scotlands Dri 14 C4
Scotlands Rd 14 B3
Seagrave Clo 15 H2
Sharpley Av 15 E2
Smith Cres 15 G3
Snipe Clo 14 A5
Speedwell Clo 14 C2
Stainsdale Grn 15 E1
Stamford Dri 15 H2
Standard Hill 14 A4
Station Rd 14 B6
Stenson Rd 14 C2
Stephenson Way 14 A1
Stone Row 14 C2
Stonehaven Clo 15 H3
Strathmore Clo 15 H3
Stretton Dri 15 H2
Swan Way 15 E4
Swithland Rd 15 G3
Sycamore Rd 15 E4
Tavistock Rd 14 B5
Teal Clo 15 E4
The Green 14 B6
The Spinney 14 A5
Thirlmere 15 G2
Thornborough Rd 14 B2
Thornton Clo 15 G3
Tiverton Av 15 E1
Torrington Av 15 E1
Totnes Rd 14 B5
Townsend La 14 A6
Tressall Rd 15 E1
Tween Town 14 A6
Twyford Clo 15 H2
Vaughan St 14 B3

Vercor Clo 15 H3
Verdon Cres 15 F2
Victoria Rd 14 C2
Vulcan Way 14 B1
Wainwright Rd 14 C5
Warren Hills Rd 15 H1
Waterworks Rd 15 E4
Welland Clo 15 E4
Wentworth Rd 14 A4
Whetstone Dri 14 C2
Whitwick Rd 14 C2
Willm Clo 15 F4
Willow Grn 15 G2
Windsor Clo 15 F3
Wolsey Rd 14 B2
Woodhouse Rd 15 F3
Woods Clo 14 B5
Wortley Clo 14 C3
Wyatt Rd 14 C2
Wyggeston Rd 14 B4
York Pl 15 H2
Zetland Clo 14 B3

HINCKLEY/ BURBAGE

Abbotts Grn 20 D1
Albert Rd 18 D4
Aldin Way 18 B2
Aldridge Rd 20 B1
Alesworth Dri 20 D2
Alexander Gdns 18 C2
Alfreton Clo 20 D1
Alma Rd 18 D4
Applebee Rd 20 A1
Argents Mead Way 18 D4
Argentsmead 18 D5
Armadale Clo 18 A4
Armour Clo 20 B2
Aran Way 18 B4
Ashburton Clo 19 G6
Ashby Ct 19 E2
Ashby Rd 18 D3
Ashford Rd 18 B5
Aster Clo 20 B1
Aster Way 20 B1
Aston La 20 E1
Atkins Way 19 E6
Aulton Cres 18 B3
Aulton Way 18 B3
Avon Walk 18 A5
Azalea Clo 20 C2
Azalea Dri 20 C2
Azalea Walk 20 C1
Baines La 18 D4
Balford Clo 19 E6
Balliol Rd 20 D1
Banky Meadow 19 G6
Baptist Walk 18 D4
Bar Mead 20 C3
Bardsey Clo 18 B4
Barlestone Dri 18 A4
Barleyfield 18 C1
Barrie Rd 18 D2
Barwell La 19 E2
Battledown Clo 18 B3
Bearsdon Cres 18 C3
Beatty Clo 18 D1
Beaumont Av 18 B6
Bedale Av 19 F2
Bedford Clo 19 E1
Beechwood Av 20 B3
Begonia Clo 20 C1
Begonia Dri 20 C1
Benbow Clo 18 D1
Beryl Av 18 A2
Blake Clo 18 D1
Blenheim Clo 19 F1
*Blockleys Yd, Regent St 18 D5
Bodmin Clo 19 F1
Bosworth Clo 18 A4
Bowling Green Rd 19 E4
Bowman Grn 20 D1
Boyslade Rd 20 C1
Boyslade Rd East 20 D2
Bradgate Rd 19 F2
Bramcote Clo 19 F2
Brame Rd 18 C3
Brandon Clo 18 C5
Brascote Rd 18 A4
Brechin Clo 18 B4
Brenfield Dri 18 B4
Briar Clo 19 F6
Bridge Clo 18 D6
Britannia Centre 18 D4
Britannia Rd 20 E2
Broadsword Way 20 B2
Brockhurst Av 20 B3
Brodick Clo 18 A4
Brodick Rd 18 A5
Brookdale 18 B5
Brookfield Rd 18 C6
Brookside 18 D6
Brosdale Dri 18 B4
Browning Dri 18 C4
Brunel Rd 18 C5
Buckingham Clo 19 F1
Bullfurlong La 20 D2
Burbage Common Rd 19 H1
Burbage Rd 19 F5
Burleigh Rd 18 C2
Burnsway 18 C4
Bute Clo 18 C3
Butt La 19 E4
Butt La Clo 19 E4
Caldon Clo 18 B5
Cambourne Rd 19 G6
Campton Clo 19 E6
Canning St 18 C4
Carpenters Clo 20 D1
Castle Ct 18 D6
Castle St 18 D4
Castlemaine Dri 19 E2
Charles St 19 E4
Charnwood Rd 19 E3
Chatsworth Clo 20 D1
Cherwell Clo 18 A5
Chesser St 18 C4
Church Clo 20 E1
Church St 20 E1
Church Walk 18 D4
Clarence Rd 19 E5
Clarendon Rd 18 C5
Cleveland Rd 18 C4
Clifton Way 18 A3
Clivesway 18 C3
Cloverfield 18 C1
Coldstream Clo 18 A4
Coley Clo 18 D5
College La 19 E4
Colts Clo 20 B3
Coppice Clo 19 F2
Coral Clo 20 D2
Cornfield 18 C1
Cornwall Way 19 E1
Cosford Dri 18 A4
Cotes Rd 20 D2
Cotman Dri 18 B2
Council Rd 18 D4
Coventry Rd, Burbage 20 C2
Coventry Rd, Hinckley 18 A6
Cowper Rd 20 B1
Crammond Clo 18 B4
Cromarty Dri 18 A4
Crossways 20 D2
Crownhill Rd 20 B3
Cumbrae Dri 18 B3
Curzon Clo 19 F6
Dahlia Clo 20 C1
Dale End Clo 18 A5
Damson Ct 18 B5
*Dares Walk, Albert Rd 18 D4
Darley Rd 20 C1
Dart Clo 18 B5
Darwin Clo 19 E1
Davenport Ter 19 E4
De Montfort Rd 19 E3
De-la-Bere Cres 20 F1
Dean Ct 19 E3
Dean Rd 19 E3
Denis Rd 20 A1
Denmore Dri 18 B3
Derby Rd 18 D3
Deveron Way 18 B3
Dorchester Rd 19 H6
Dove Clo 18 A5
Drake Way 18 D1
Druid Pl 18 D4
Druid St 18 D4
Dudley Rise 18 D6
Dunblane Way 18 B3
Duport Rd 19 F5
East Clo 18 D6
Eastwoods Rd 19 F3
Edale Grn 20 D1
Edendale Dri 19 E1
Edward Rd 18 C2
Elizabeth Rd 18 D2
Elm Tree Dri 19 F5
Embleton Clo 18 B4
Erskine Clo 18 A3
Eskdale Rd 18 A5
Factory Rd 18 D3
Fairways Ct 19 G2
Falconers Grn 20 D1
Falmouth Dri 19 E1
Far Lash 19 F6
Farm Rd 20 C1
Farneway 18 B4
Farriers Way 20 D1
Featherston Dri 18 D6
Ferness Clo 18 B3
Ferness Rd 18 B3
Field Clo 19 F1
Flamville Rd 20 F2
Fletcher Rd 19 E6
Forrest Rd 19 F5
Forresters Clo 19 F6
Forresters Clo 20 D1
Forresters Rd 20 D1
Forryan Rd 19 F6
Frederick Av 18 B2
Freemans La 20 E2
Friary Clo 19 E4
Frith Way 18 A2
Frobisher Clo 18 D1
Gabden Rd 18 D3
Gainsborough Av 18 A2
Garden Clo 18 D6
George St 18 D5
Gladstone Clo 19 E1
Gladstone Ter 19 E4
Glebe Rd 19 F4
Glen Bank 19 E4
Glenbarr Clo 18 A4
Glenbarr Dri 18 A4
Goosehills Rd 20 C2
Gopal Rd 18 D3
Gowrie Clo 18 B3
Granby Clo 18 C5
Granby Rd 18 C5
Grange Dri 20 C2
Granville Gdns 18 C5
Greenmoor Rd 20 B1
Grosvenor Cres 20 E1
Grove Park 20 E1
Grove Rd 20 E1
Gwendoline Av 18 A2
Halbert Clo 20 B2
Hall Rd 20 B1
Hamilton Clo 18 B3
Hangmans La 19 E1
Hanover Ct 20 C1
Hansom Ct 18 D4
Hanson Rd 19 F3
Hardy Clo 19 D1
Hartington Grn 20 C1
Harwood Dri 19 F1
Hawkins Clo 18 D1
Hawley Rd 18 D6
Hawthorn Cres 20 C2
Hays La 18 B5
Henry St 18 A2
Hereford Way 19 F6
Herlad Way 20 B2
Higham Way 19 E6
Highfields Rd 19 E4
Hill St 19 E4
Hillrise 19 F5
Hillside Rd 20 B1
Hinckley Rd 19 G6
Hogarth Clo 18 A2
Hogarth Dri 18 A2
Holliers Walk 18 D4
Holly Clo 20 C2
Hollycroft 18 C3
Hollycroft Cres 18 C3
Holt Rd 19 E6
Horsepool 20 E1
Hurst Rd 18 D5
Hyacinth Way 20 B1
Ilminster Clo 19 H6
INDUSTRIAL ESTATES:
Nutts La Trading Est 18 A6
Sapcote Rd Ind Est 19 G5
Sketchley La Ind Est 20 A2
Sketchley Meadows Business Park 20 A2
Iris Clo 20 C2
Island Clo 19 E3
Jarvis Clo 18 D1
Jefferies Clo 19 E3
Jelicoe Way 18 D1
John Nichols St 18 B6
John St 19 E3
Johns Clo 20 B2
Kent Dri 19 E1
Kestrel Clo 20 D1
Kilberry Clo 18 A3
Kilby Grn 20 D1
Kilmarie Clo 18 A4
King Georges Way 18 B6
King Richard Rd 18 C3
King St 18 D4
Kingston Dri 19 E1
Kinros Way 18 A4
Kintyre Clo 18 B3
Kirfield Dri 19 F2
Knapton Clo 18 A2
Knights Clo 20 B2
Lancaster Rd 18 D5
Lance Clo 20 B2
Landseer Dri 18 B2
Laneside Clo 19 F1
Laneside Dri 19 F2
Langdale Rd 18 A5
Lash Hill Path 19 F6
Lawns Wood 18 A5
Lawton Clo 18 A4
Leicester Rd 19 E4
Leven Clo 18 B4
Library Clo 20 E2
Lilac Clo 20 C1
Linden Rd 18 C4
Linwood Clo 18 B3
Lismore Dri 18 C3
Lobelia Clo 20 C1
Lochmore Clo 18 A4
Lochmore Dri 18 A4
Lochmore Way 18 A4
Lodge Clo 20 E2
Lomond Clo 18 B4
London Rd 19 E4
Love La 20 E1
Lower Bond St 18 D4
Lucas Rd 20 B1
Lundy Clo 18 B4
Lupin Clo 20 B1
Lutterworth Rd 20 E2
Lychgate Clo 20 E2
Lychgate La 20 E2
Lyndhurst Clo 19 G6
Lyneham Clo 18 B4
Magee Clo 18 D2
Maizefield 18 C1
Manor Clo 20 A2
Manor Pl 18 D4
Manor St 18 D4
Manor Way 20 B2
Mansion St 18 D4
Maple Clo 20 C2
Marchant Rd 18 C5
Marigold Dri 20 C2
Market Pl 18 D4
Marlborough Clo 19 G6
Mason Ct 18 C5
Meadow Dri 19 G6
Melrose Clo 18 B4
Merevale Av 18 C5
Merrick Ct 20 D2
Merrifield Gdns 20 C2
Middlefield Clo 18 D3
Middlefield Ct 18 D3
Middlefield La 18 D2
Middlefield Pl 18 D2
Mill Hill Rd 18 C4
Mill View 19 E4
Millais Rd 18 B2
Millers Grn 20 D1
Milton Clo 18 C4
Moray Clo 18 B4
Morland Dri 18 B2
Mount Rd 18 D5
Nelson Dri 19 D1
Netherley Rd 18 D2
New Bldgs 18 D4
New Rd 20 E1
New St 18 D3
Newquay Clo 19 E1
Newstead Av 20 B3
Norfolk Clo 20 C3
North Clo 20 C1
Northern Perimeter Rd West 18 A2
Northfield Rd 18 C5
Norwood Clo 19 F1
Nutts La 18 A6
Oaks Clo 20 C2
Oban Rd 18 A6
Orchard Clo 20 E2
Orchard St 19 E4
Orkney Clo 18 C4
Osbaston Clo 19 F2
Outlands Dri 18 A3
Paddock La 20 D2
Palmer Rd 18 B3
Park Rd 19 E5
Parsons La 19 E5
Pennant Rd 20 B2
Pentland Clo 18 B4
Penzance Clo 19 E1
Pike Clo 20 B2
Pilgrims Gate 20 E1
Portland Dri 19 E
Preston Rd 18 B
Priesthills Rd 18 D
Primrose Dri 20 C
Princess Rd 19 E
Priory Walk 19 E
Pughes Clo 20 E
Pyeharps Rd 20 C
Queens Park Ter 19 E
Queens Rd 19 E
Radmore Rd 18 D
Raleigh Clo 18 D
Ramsey Clo 18 B
Rannoch Clo 18 B
Ratcliffe Rd 20 D
Reeves Rd 20 D
Regency Ct 19 G
*Regent Ct, Regent St 18 D
Regent St 18 D
Ribblesdale Av 19 E
Richmond Rd 18 C
Riddon Dri 18 B
Robinson Way 20 D
Rodney Clo 18 D
Romney Clo 18 A
Rosemary Way 18 B
Rosewood Clo 19 F
Roston Dri 18 A
Royal Ct 18 D
Rufford Clo 20 B
Rugby Rd 18 C
Rutland Av 18 C
Rydale Clo 18 A
Saddlers Clo 20 D
St Catherine Clo 19 F
St Georges Av 18 C
St James Clo 20 B
St Martins 20 B
St Marys Rd 18 D
St Pauls Gdn 19 E
Salem Rd 20 D
Salisbury Rd 19 G
Sandy Cres 18 C
Sandy Walk 18 B
Sapcote Rd 19 G
Saville Clo 19 E
School Clo 20 E
Seaforth Dri 18 A
Seaton Clo 19 G
Severn Av 18 B
Shakespeare Dri 18 C
Sharpless Rd 19 E
Shelley Gdns 19 E
Sherborne Rd 19 H
Sisley Way 18 B
Sketchley Hall Gdns 20 A
Sketchley La 20 A
Sketchley Manor La 20 B
Sketchley Meadows 20 A
Sketchley Old Village 20 B
Sketchley Rd 20 C
Soarway 18 A
Southfield Rd 18 D
Spa Clo 19 E
Spa La 19 E
Spencer St 18 D
Spinney Rd 20 A
Springfield Rd 18 D
Squires Grn 20 D
Stanley Rd 18 C
Station Rd 18 D
Stirling Av 18 A
Stockwell Head 18 D
Stoke Rd 18 B
Stoneygate Dri 19 E
Strathmore Rd 18 A
Stretton Clo 20 B
Strutt Rd 20 E
Sunnydale Cres 18 A
Sunnydale Rd 18 A
Sunnyhill 19 F
Sunnyhill Sth 19 F
Sunnyside 19 E
Sunnyside Park 18 D
Surrey Clo 20 C
Sutton Clo 19 F
Swains Grn 20 D
Swinburne Rd 18 C
Sycamore Clo 20 C
Tame Way 18 A
Teign Bank Clo 18 D
Teign Bank Rd 18 D
Tennyson Rd 18 C
The Borough 18 D
The Butwoods 19 F
The Coppice 19 F
The Fairway 19 F
The Grove 18 C
The Horse Fair 18 D

e Lawns 19 E4
e Meadow 19 F5
e Meadows 19 G6
ne Narrows, Hill St 19 E4
e Ridgeway 20 B1
e Rills 19 E3
e Spindles 20 D2
rlmere Rd 18 A5
ornfield Way 19 E5
orny Croft Rd 19 E5
ee Pots Rd 20 C3
on Rd 20 C1
ridon Way 18 B3
fford Rd 19 F3
ent Av 18 B5
ent Rd 18 A5
evor Rd 19 F4
nity La 18 C5
nity Vicarage Rd 18 C4
uro Clo 19 E1
dor Rd 18 C2
rner Dri 18 A2
eedside Clo 19 F1
ycross Rd 20 D1
per Bond St 18 D4
ctoria Rd 20 D2
ctoria St 19 E3
la Clo 20 D2
alney Clo 18 B3
arwick Gdns 19 E1
aterfield Way 20 A2
aterloo Rd 18 D5
atling Clo 20 A2
atling St 20 A3
aveney Clo 18 B5
elbeck Av 20 B3
ell La 18 D4
elwyn Rd 19 F4
endover Dri 19 E1
ensum Clo 18 B5
entworth Clo 19 E2
esley Walk 20 E1
est Clo 18 D6
estfield Ct 18 C6
estfield Rd 18 C6
estminster Dri 20 D2
eston Clo 18 B4
estray Dri 18 C4
heatfield Way 18 C1
illiam Iliffe St 18 B6
illow Clo 20 C2
illowbank Clo 18 C5
illowdale 18 B5
inchester Dri 19 G6
indrush Dri 18 A5
indsor Ct 20 E2
indsor St 20 E2
oburn Clo 19 E1
olvey Rd 20 C3
ood St 18 D4
ood St Clo 19 E4
oodfield Rd 20 A1
oodgate Rd 19 F5
oodland Av 19 G6
oodland Rd 19 F3
oodstock Clo 20 E1
oolbank 19 G6
orkhouse La 20 E2
ye Clo 18 A5
ykin Rd 18 A2
ork Rd 18 D2
ealand Clo 19 F1

IBSTOCK

bert St 17 B1
gyle St 17 B1
shby Rd 17 A1
shdale 17 A2
eech Way 17 A2
ernard Clo 17 B3
rookside Cres 17 B2
edar Dri 17 A2
entral Av 17 B2
hapel St 17 B2
hestnut Clo 17 A2
hristopher Clo 17 B1
hurch View 17 A3
opson St 17 B3
ostello Clo 17 C1
ross Clo 17 B3
urzon St 17 B2
eepdale Clo 17 B2
ouglas Dri 17 B3
ast Walk 17 B2
izabeth Av 17 B1
m Clo 17 A2
Fairfield 17 B3
Ferndale 17 A2
Gamble Clo 17 B1
Gladstone St 17 B3
Glen Av 17 B3
Grange Rd 17 B3
Hall St 17 A3
Harrats Clo 17 B3
Hawthorne Dri 17 A3
Heatherdale 17 A2
High St 17 A3
Hinckley Rd 17 A3
Jacques Rd 17 B1
Laud Clo 17 A3
Legion Dri 17 B3
Leicester Rd 17 B2
Linden Clo 17 A2
Maple Dri 17 A2
Meadow Walk 17 B2
Melbourne Rd 17 A3
Oak Dri 17 A2
Orchard St 17 B3
Paget Rd 17 B1
Parkdale 17 A2
Penistone St 17 B1
Pretoria Rd 17 C2
Ravenstone Rd 17 B1
Redlands Est 17 C1
Reform St 17 A3
Rowan Dri 17 A2
St Denys Cres 17 A3
Slaybarns Way 17 B2
Spring Rd 17 C2
Springfield Clo 17 B2
Station Rd 17 A2
Sunnyside 17 A3
Swifts Clo 17 B2
Sycamore Clo 17 A2
The Hastings 17 B2
Thorndale 17 A3
Thornham Gro 17 B2
Valley Rd 17 A3
Victoria Rd 17 B1
West Walk 17 B2
Willow Way 17 A2
Winchester Ct 17 B1

KEGWORTH

Bedford Clo 17 B6
Borough St 17 B5
Borrowell 17 B4
Bradhill Rd 17 B5
Bridge Fields 17 C5
Bulstode Pl 17 B5
Burley Rise 17 B6
Citrus Gro 17 B4
Derby Rd 17 A4
Dragwell 17 B5
Foxhills 17 A6
Frederick Av 17 B4
Gerrard Cres 17 B6
Heafield Dri 17 B5
High St 17 A5
Hillside 17 B6
Kingston La 17 D4
Kirby Dri 17 B6
Kirk Av 17 C5
Langley Dri 17 A5
Leatherlands 17 B5
London Rd 17 C6
Long La 17 B4
Mill La 17 C5
Moore Av 17 C4
New Brickyard La 17 B6
New St 17 C4
Nine Acres 17 A5
Norman Ct 17 B6
Nottingham Rd 17 B4
Oldershaw Av 17 B5
Packington Hill 17 A4
Peppers Dri 17 A5
Pleasant Pl 17 B5
Plummer La 17 B5
Queens Rd 17 B5
Roberts Clo 17 B6
Ropewalk 17 B5
St Andrews Rd 17 B6
Shepherd Walk 17 B6
Sibson Dri 17 A5
Side Lea 17 B4
Springfied 17 A5
Staffords Acres 17 B5
Station Rd 17 C4
Stone Hills 17 A5
Suthers Rd 17 A5
Sutton Rd 17 B6
The Croft 17 B5
The Osiers 17 C5
Thomas Rd 17 B6
Walton Ct 17 B5
West Bank Mews 17 A5
Whatton Rd 17 A6
Windmill Way 17 A5
Wyvelle Cres 17 B4

LEICESTER CITY CENTRE

Abbey St 21 B2
Abbey Walk 21 B1
Albion St 21 C4
Alfred Pl 21 C4
All Saints Open 21 A2
All Saints Rd 21 A3
Andover St 21 D5
Ann St 21 D3
Apple Gate 21 A4
Archdeacon La 21 C1
Arnhem St 21 D5
Ashwell St 21 D5
Atkins St 21 B6
Barston St 21 B1
Bath La 21 A4
Bay St 21 B1
Bedford St Nth 21 C1
Bedford St Sth 21 C2
Belgrave Gate 21 C1
Belvoir St 21 C4
Berkley St 21 A2
Berridge St 21 B4
Bishop St 21 C4
Blake St 21 B2
Bonners La 21 B5
Bowling Green St 21 B4
Bowmars La 21 A1
Britannia St 21 C1
Brougham St 21 D2
Burgess St 21 A2
Burleys Flyover 21 C1
Burleys Way 21 B2
Burton St 21 D3
Butt Clo La 21 B2
Byron St 21 C3
Calais Hill 21 C5
Calais St 21 C5
Calgary Rd 21 D1
Camden St 21 C3
Campbell St 21 D4
Cank St 21 B4
Canning Pl 21 B1
Canning St 21 B1
Careys Clo 21 A4
Carlton St 21 B6
Carts La 21 B3
Castle St 21 A4
Castle View 21 A5
Castle Yard 21 A4
Causeway La 21 A3
Chancery St 21 B4
Charles St 21 C3
Charter St 21 C1
Chatham St 21 C5
Cheapside 21 B3
Christow St 21 D2
Church Gate 21 B2
Church St 21 D4
Clarence St 21 C3
Clarendon St 21 A6
Clyde St 21 D2
Colton St 21 C4
Conduit St 21 D5
Constitution Hill 21 D4
Crafton St East 21 D2
Crafton St West 21 D2
Crane St 21 B2
Craven St 21 A1
Crescent St 21 C6
Cumberland St 21 A2
Darker St 21 B2
De Montfort Mews 21 D6
De Montfort Pl 21 D6
De Montfort Sq 21 D6
De Montfort St 21 D6
Deacon St 21 A6
Devonshire St 21 B1
Dover St 21 C5
Dryden St 21 C2
Duke St 21 B5
Dunkirk St 21 C5
Earl St 21 C3
East Bond St 21 B2
East Gates 21 B3
East St 21 C5
Eastern Boulevard 21 A6
Edmonton Rd 21 D2
Elbow La 21 A2
Eldon St 21 C3
Erskine St 21 D3
Every St 21 C4
Fleet St 21 C2
Foundry La 21 C1
Fox La 21 C3
Fox St 21 D4
Fraser Clo 21 D1
Free La 21 C3
Freeschool La 21 A3
Friar La 21 A4
Friars Causeway 21 A3
Friday St 21 A1
Gallowtree Gate 21 B3
Garden St 21 C2
Gas St 21 C1
Gateway St 21 A5
George St 21 C1
Gladstone St 21 D2
Glebe St 21 D4
Gosling St 21 A5
Gower St 21 C2
Grafton Pl 21 B1
Granby Pl 21 C4
Granby St 21 C4
Grange La 21 B5
Grape St 21 B2
Grasmere St 21 A6
Gravel St 21 B2
Gray St 21 A5
Great Central St 21 A2
Greyfriars 21 B4
Grosvenor St 21 C1
Guildhall La 21 A4
Halford St 21 C4
Hannah Ct 21 C3
Harding St 21 A1
Harveys Walk 21 A4
Havelock St 21 A6
Haymarket 21 B3
Heanor St 21 A1
Henshaw St 21 B6
High St 21 A3
Highcross St 21 A2
Hill St 21 C3
Holy Bones 21 A3
Horsefair St 21 B4
Hotel St 21 B4
Humberstone Gate 21 B3
Humberstone Rd 21 D3
Infirmary Clo 21 B6
Infirmary Rd 21 B6
Infirmary Sq 21 B6
Jarrom St 21 A6
Johnson St 21 A1
Jubilee Rd 21 C2
Junction Rd 21 D1
Junior St 21 A2
Kamloops Cres 21 D1
Kildare St 21 C3
King St 21 B5
Labrador Clo 21 D2
Langton St 21 C2
Lee Circle 21 C2
Lethbridge Clo 21 D2
Lichfield St 21 B2
London Rd 21 D5
Long La 21 A2
Loseby La 21 B4
Lower Brown St 21 B5
Lower Free La 21 C3
Lower Garden St 21 C2
Lower Hastings St 21 C6
Lower Hill Rd 21 C2
Lower Lee St 21 C2
Mackenzie Way 21 D1
Magazine Walk 21 A5
Malcolm Arc 21 B3
Manitoba Rd 21 D2
Mansfield St 21 B2
Marble St 21 B4
Market Pl 21 B4
Market Pl App 21 C4
Market Pl Sth 21 B4
Market St 21 B4
Marlborough St 21 B5
Marquis St 21 C5
Melton St 21 C1
Memory La 21 C1
Midland St 21 D3
Mill La 21 A6
Mill St 21 B5
Millstone La 21 B4
Monckton Clo 21 D1
Montreal Rd 21 D1
Morgan Ct 21 A3
Morledge St 21 D3
Museum Sq 21 C5
Navigation St 21 C1
Needlegate 21 A2
Nelson St 21 D5
New Bond St 21 B3
New Parliament St 21 C2
New Rd 21 B2
New St 21 B4
New Walk 21 C5
Newarke Clo 21 A5
Newarke St 21 B5
Newport Pl 21 C4
Newtown St 21 C6
Nichols St 21 D3
Northampton Sq 21 C4
Northampton St 21 C4
Northgate St 21 A2
Northgates 21 A2
Northumberland St 21 A2
Norton St 21 B5
Odeon Arc 21 B4
Old Mill La 21 A2
Old Milton St 21 C2
Ontario Clo 21 D1
Orchard St 21 C2
Ottawa Rd 21 D2
Oxford St 21 B5
Pares St 21 B1
Park St 21 C5
Pasture La 21 A2
Peacock La 21 A4
Pelham St 21 B6
Pelham Way 21 B6
Pocklingtons Walk 21 B4
Potter St 21 D3
Prebend St 21 D5
Princess Rd East 21 D6
Princess Rd West 21 C5
Quebec Rd 21 D2
Queen St 21 D3
Rawson St 21 C6
Regent Rd 21 B5
Regent St 21 D5
Richmond St 21 A5
Royal Arc 21 B3
Royal East St 21 C2
Rupert St 21 B4
Russell Sq 21 D1
Rutland St 21 C4
Rydal St 21 A6
St Augustine Rd 21 A4
St George St 21 D4
St Georges Way 21 D4
St James St 21 C3
St John St 21 B1
St Margarets St 21 B2
St Margarets Way 21 A1
St Mark St 21 C1
St Martins 21 B4
St Martins East 21 A4
St Martins West 21 A4
St Matthews Way 21 C2
St Nicholas Circle 21 A4
St Nicholas Pl 21 A4
St Peters La 21 A3
Samuel St 21 D3
Sandacre St 21 B2
Sanvey Gate 21 A2
*Shackleton St, Woodboy St 21 C1
Shires La 21 B3
Short St 21 B2
Silver Arc 21 B3
Silver St 21 B3
Slate St 21 D5
Slater St 21 A1
Soar La 21 A2
South Albion St 21 C5
South Church Gate 21 B1
Southampton St 21 D3
Southgates 21 A4
Stamford St 21 C4
Station St 21 D5
Swain St 21 D4
Talbot La 21 A4
Taylor Rd 21 D1
Thames St 21 C1
The Crescent 21 C5
The Gateway 21 A5
The Newarke 21 A5
The Oval 21 D6
Thornton Walk 21 A4
Toronto Clo 21 D1
Tower St 21 C6
Trinity La 21 C6
Turner St 21 C6
Ullswater St 21 A6
Upper Brown St 21 B5
Upper George St 21 D1

Street	Ref
Wartnaby St	27 A5
Warwick Clo	26 D3
Waterfield Pl	26 C3
Watson Av	27 A7
Welham Rd	26 E2
Welland Park Rd	27 B6
Western Av	27 B7
Westfield Clo	27 A5
Willow Cres	27 A6
Wilson Clo	27 E5
Windsor Ct	26 B4
Woburn Clo	27 E5
Worcester Dri	26 C3
York St	27 D5

MEASHAM

Abney Cres	25 B2
Abney Dri	25 B3
Abney Walk	25 B2
Ash Dri	25 C1
Ashby Rd	25 C1
Atherstone Rd	25 B2
Blackthorne Way	25 B1
Bleach Hill	25 B3
Bosworth Rd	25 C1
Browning Dri	25 B3
Buckley Clo	25 C2
Burns Clo	25 B3
Burton Rd	25 A1
Byron Cres	25 B3
Chapel St	25 B1
Cophills Clo	25 B2
Dryden Clo	25 B3
Dysons Clo	25 A2
Fenton Clo	25 B3
Fenton Cres	25 B3
Gallows La	25 D3
Grassy La	25 D1
Greenfield Rd	25 D1
Hawthorne Clo	25 B1
Hazel Clo	25 B1
High St	25 B2
Holly Rd	25 C1
Horses La	25 C2
Huntington Ct	25 A2
Huntington Way	25 A1
Iveagh Clo	25 C1
Jewsbury Av	25 D2
Leicester Rd	25 C1
Lime Av	25 B1
Mannings Ter	25 B2
Masefield Clo	25 B3
Meadow Gdns	25 B3
Mease Clo	25 B3
Milton Clo	25 B3
Navigation St	25 C2
New St	25 C1
Oak Clo	25 B1
Orchard Way	25 B1
Peggs Clo	25 C2
Poplar Dri	25 C1
Queens St	25 C1
Repton Rd	25 A2
River Way	25 A3
Riverside Ct	25 A2
Rowan Clo	25 B1
Sandhill Clo	25 B2
Shackland Dri	25 D2
Shelley Clo	25 B3
Tamworth Rd	25 A3
Tennyson Clo	25 B3
The Croft	25 A2
Uplands Rd	25 B2
Wesley Hillman Ct	25 C2
Wilkes Av	25 B2
Willow Clo	25 C1
Wordsworth Way	25 B3
York Clo	25 B1

MELTON MOWBRAY

Abingdon Rd	28 B2
Acres Rise	28 F3
Adcock Clo	28 F2
Albert St	29 D6
Algernon Rd	28 E4
Alvaston Rd	29 D6
Ankle Hill Rd	29 D6
Arden Dri	28 A3
Ash Gro	28 C3
Ashfordby Rd	28 A4
Ashton Clo	29 C6
Avon Rd	29 C6
Baldocks La	29 D5
Balmoral Rd	28 C2
Banbury Dri	29 E7
Barker Cres	29 C7
Barngate Clo	28 D2
Bayswater Rd	28 B4
Beaconsfield Rd	28 D2
Beaumont Gdns	28 D2
Beck Hill Ct	28 B4
Belvoir St	28 E3
Bentley St	28 D4
Bickley Av	28 D3
Birch Clo	28 C3
Bishop St	28 E4
Blakeney Cres	29 C7
Blenheim Walk	28 C2
Blythe Av	29 B5
Bowley Av	28 E2
Brampton Rd	28 A1
Branston Cres	29 E5
Brentingsby Clo	29 E5
Breward Way	28 D1
Brightside Av	28 B4
Brocklehurst Rd	28 F2
Brook La	29 D5
Brook St	28 D4
Brookfield Ct	28 B2
Brookfield St	28 B2
Browning Clo	28 D4
Brownlow Cres	29 C7
Buckminster Clo	29 E5
Burns Clo	28 C1
Burton Rd	28 D4
Burton St	29 D5
Byron Way	28 C1
Cambridge Av	29 D7
Canterbury Dri	28 A1
Carnegie Cres	28 F2
Cedar Dri	28 C3
Chadwell Clo	29 E5
Chalfont Clo	29 E7
Chalmondley Dri	28 D1
Chapel St	28 D4
Charlotte St	28 C4
Charnwood Dri	28 A3
Cheapside	28 C4
Chestnut Way	29 C6
Chetwynd Dri	28 A4
Cholmondley St	28 D1
Church St	28 D4
Churchill Clo	28 D2
Clark Dri	28 D2
Clumber St	28 C3
College Av	29 D6
Collingwood Cres	28 A4
Coniston Rd	28 A1
Conway Dri	28 C2
Copley Clo	28 E3
Cornwall Pl	29 C7
Cotswold Clo	29 E7
Cottesmore Av	28 C4
Cranmere Rd	28 D2
Craven St	29 D6
Crossfield Dri	28 F3
Dalby Rd	29 C5
De Montford	28 C2
Delamare Rd	28 D1
Denton Rise	29 E5
Derwent Dri	28 C1
Dickens Dri	28 C1
Dieppe Way	28 E3
Doctors La	28 E3
Dorian Rise	29 C5
Dorothy Av	28 B4
Dorset Dri	29 D7
Douglas Jane Clo	28 B3
Dovedale Clo	29 C6
Drive Dalby Rd	28 C2
Drummond Walk	28 C2
Duke St	28 E3
Dulverton Rd	28 B2
Eagles Dri	29 C7
East Av	28 B3
East Side Croft	28 C4
Eastfield Av	28 D3
Edendale Rd	29 B6
Egerton Rd	28 D4
Egerton View	29 C5
Elgin Dri	28 C3
Elmhurst Av	28 A2
Elms Rd	28 D2
Epping Dri	28 A2
Everest Dri	29 C6
Ewden Rise	29 E5
Fairfield Clo	28 D2
Faldo Dri	28 D1
Farmland Clo	28 D1
Ferneley Cres	28 E3
Fernie Av	28 C4
Field Clo	29 E6
Firwood Rd	28 E2
Forest Clo	28 D2
Freeby Clo	29 F5
Freshney Clo	29 B6
Garden La	28 B2
Garthorpe Dri	29 E5
Gartree Ct	29 D6
Gartree Dri	29 D6
Gaudaloupe Av	29 F6
George St	28 E4
Gilpin Clo	29 B6
Gladstone Av	28 B2
Gloucester Av	29 D7
Gloucester Cres	29 D7
Golds Pink Clo	29 C7
Granby Rd	28 D1
Grange Dri	29 E5
Grantwood Rd	28 E2
Granville Rd	28 B2
Greaves Av	28 B3
Green Bank	28 E4
Greenhill Clo	28 D2
Greenslade	28 D4
Gretton Ct	28 B4
Hadfield Dri	28 D3
Hamilton Dri	29 C6
Harlech Way	28 C2
Hartland Dri	29 C6
Hartopp Rd	29 C7
Hawthorn Dri	28 C2
High St	28 C4
Highfield Av	28 B2
Hillside Av	28 B2
Hollygate Clo	29 F5
Hudson Rd	29 F3
Humber Dri	29 C6
Hunt Dri	28 F2
Hunters Rd	29 D5

INDUSTRIAL ESTATES:

Hudson Rd Ind Est	28 F4

Street	Ref
Irwell Clo	29 B6
James Lambert Dri	28 A2
Jarvis Dri	28 B3
Johnson Clo	28 D3
Jubilee St	28 D4
Jubilee Way	28 E2
Kapelle Clo	28 F2
Keats Clo	28 C2
Kennet Way	29 B6
Kestrel Clo	29 C7
King St	28 D4
Kings Av	28 E3
Kings Rd	28 D4
Kipling Dri	28 B2
Kirby La	29 A7
Kirton Dri	28 B1
Lake Ter	29 B5
Lambert Clo	28 D2
Laycock Av	28 C3
Leicester Rd	29 A6
Leicester St	28 C3
Lilac Way	28 C3
Limes Av	28 E3
Lincoln Dri	29 D7
Linnet Clo	29 B7
Loddon Clo	29 B6
Longate Rd	28 D2
Longfield Rd	28 D2
Longwill Av	28 D3
Lowesey Clo	29 F5
Loxley Dri	29 B6
Ludlow Dri	28 C2
Lyle Clo	28 B4
Lynton Rd	28 D1
Manners Clo	28 B2
Manor Clo	28 F2
Maple Clo	28 C2
Market Pl	28 D4
Marteg Clo	29 B6
Mayfield St	28 B2
Meadow Way	29 E6
Medway Dri	29 C6
Melbourne St	28 A4
Melbray Dri	28 C1
Melton Spinney Rd	28 F2
Meynell Clo	29 C7
Mildmay Clo	28 D1
Mill La	29 D5
Mill St	29 D5
Milton Clo	28 C2
Morley St	28 A3
Mortimer Rd	28 D3
Mowbray Ct	29 B5
Needham Clo	28 D3
Nene Clo	29 B5
New St	28 D4
Newbury Av	28 E3
Newport Av	28 C3
Norfolk Dri	29 D7
Norman Way	28 C4
North St	28 D4
Northfield Clo	28 C3
Nottingham Rd	28 A1
Nottingham St	28 C4
Oak Rd	28 D4
Old Bridewell	28 D2
Owen Cres	28 D3
Oxford Dri	29 D7
Paddock Clo	29 D6
Pall Mall	28 F2
Palmerston Rd	28 B2
Park Av	28 B4
Park La	28 C4
Park Rd	28 C4
Pebble Bank La	28 F3
Petersfield Rd	28 B3
Pochin Clo	29 B6
Pollard Clo	28 F2
Princess Dri	29 C7
Queensway	29 C7
Quorn Av	28 B4
Raynes Walk	28 D3
Redbrook Cres	29 B6
Redwood Av	28 D2
Regent Pl	29 D5
Regent St	29 D5
Ribble Way	29 C6
Richmond Dri	29 E7
Riverside Rd	28 A4
Robin Cres	29 B7
Rockingham St	28 B3
Roseberry Av	28 D4
Ross Clo	28 E2
Rudbeck Av	28 B4
Rutland St	28 D4
Sage Cross St	28 D4
St Johns Ct	28 D4
St Johns St	28 C2
St Marys Clo	28 C4
Salisbury Av	28 E3
Sandy La	29 D6
Sapcote Dri	29 E6
Saxby Rd	28 E4
Scalford Rd	28 C1
Severn Hill	29 C6
Shelley Av	28 C2
Sherrard St	28 D4
Sherwood Dri	28 A4
Snow Hill	28 D4
Soar Clo	29 B6
Solway Clo	29 B6
Somerset Clo	28 D7
South Par	28 C4
Spinney Clo	28 F2
Springfield St	28 B3
Stafford Av	28 E4
Stanley St	28 D4
Staveley Rd	28 A3
Stirling Rd	28 B3
Sussex Av	29 D7
Swale Clo	28 C3
Swallowdale Rd	29 C7
Swan Clo	29 B7
Swift Clo	29 C7
Sycamore Clo	28 C3
Sysonby Grange La	28 A4
Sysonby St	28 B3
Tamar Rd	29 B6
Tennis Av	29 F5
Tennyson Way	28 C2
Thames Dri	28 C2
The Crescent	28 C3
The Uplands	28 B2
Thorpe End	28 D4
Thorpe Rd	28 E4
Thrush Clo	29 B7
Torrance Dri	28 D1
Trent Bank	29 B6
Tudor Hill	29 D7
Tweed Dri	29 C6
Valley Rd	29 B6
Victoria St	29 D6
Waltham Rise	29 E5
Warwick Rd	29 C7
Waverley Ct	29 C7
Weaver Grn	29 C6
Welby La	28 D1
Welland Rise	28 C2
West Av	28 B3
Westminster Clo	28 A3
Whitelake Clo	29 B6
Wicklow Av	29 D6
Willcox Dri	29 B5
Willoughby Clo	29 B5
Willow Dri	28 D4
Wilton Ct	28 A2
Wilton Rd	28
Wilton Ter	28
Winchester Dri	28
Windsor St	28
Winster Cres	29
Witham Clo	29
Woodcock Dri	29
Woodland Av	29
Worcester Dri	28
Wren Clo	29
Wycliffe Av	29
Wycomb Gro	29
Wyfordby Clo	29
Wymondham Way	28
Wyndham Av	29
Wyvern Ter	28
Yew Tree Cres	28

NARBOROUGH ENDERBY

Abbey Rd	31
Acan Way	31
Acer Clo	31
Alexander Av	30
Alexandra St	31
Alyssum Way	31
Aquitane Clo	30
Ashlands Way	31
Badgers Clo	31
Bantlam La	30
Barbara Clo	30
Beechwood Rd	31
Beggars La	30
Bell La	31
Belle View	31
Bennett Rise	31
Biddle Rd	31
Bingley Ct	31
Bingley Rd	31
Blake Ct	30
Blakenhall Clo	31
Boswell St	31
Briers Clo	31
Broad St	30
Brook St, Enderby	30
Brook St, Huncote	31
Broom Way	31
Broomhills Rd	31
Browning St	31
Burns St	31
Burrows Clo	31
Bushey Clo	31
Buttercup Clo	31
Byron Clo	30
Callan Clo	31
Camellia Clo	31
Camelot Way	30
Campion Clo	31
Canons Clo	31
Capers Clo	30
Carey Rd	31
Carlton Av	31
Carter Clo	30
Cedar Cres	31
Chantry Clo	31
Chapel St	30
Chaucer St	31
Cheney End	31
Cherrytree Gro	30
Chestnut Clo	31
Cheyney Ct	31
Church La	31
Church View	31
Clover Clo	31
Coleridge Dri	30
Coltbeck Av	31
Columbia Rd	30
Compton Dri	31
Conery La	30
Cooper Clo	31
Cooperation St	30
Copt Oak Clo	31
Copt Oak Rd	31
Cornfield Clo	31
Cornwall St	30
Cosby Rd	31
Coventry Clo	31
Coventry Rd	31
Cowslip Clo	31
Critchlow Rd	31
Cross St	30
Cumberwell Dri	30
Cutters Clo	31
Denman La	31
Desford Rd, Enderby	30

OAKHAM

RATBY/ KIRBY MUXLOE

47

The Close	33 A2	Halstead Rd	34 A3
The Croft	33 B5	Hawcliffe Rd	34 B1
The Fairway	33 C6	Hawthorn Rd	34 C2
The Huntings	33 A5	Heron Clo	34 C2
The Keep	33 B5	Highfields Rd	34 B3
The Mill La	33 D2	Homefield La	34 D5
The Oasts	33 D3	Horne Croft	34 C5
Timberwood Dri	33 B1	Howe La	34 C6
Towers Dri	33 B6	Iris Clo	34 C2
Tudor Gro	33 C1	Johns Av	34 C3
Tyler Rd	33 B3	Kenilworth Clo	34 B3
Ulverscroft Dri	33 C1	Kestrel La	34 D2
Vicarage Clo	33 C4	Kinchley La	34 A3
Victoria Dri	33 C1	Kingfisher Rd	34 C2
Walton Clo	33 C6	Kirby Clo	34 B4
Wanstead Rd	33 D5	Knights Cres	34 C5
Warrington Dri	33 B1	Laurel Clo	34 C2
Wentworth Grn	33 B6	Leicester Rd	34 B2
Wesley Clo	33 A3	Linden Gro	34 C3
Whitehouse Clo	33 B1	Linkfield Av	34 C3
Whittington Dri	33 A2	Linkfield Rd	34 C3
Willow Dri	33 B1	Long Furlong	34 B4
Wilshere Clo	33 A6	Loughborough Rd,	
Windmill Clo	33 B3	Mountsorell	34 D3
Windsor Av	33 C1	Loughborough Rd,	
Wollaton Clo	33 D3	North End	34 B1
Wolsey Clo	33 C1	Macaulay Rd	34 C5
Woodlands La	33 B4	Maitland Av	34 C3
Woodley Rd	33 A2	Mallard Rd	34 U2
		Marigold La	34 C2
		Market Pl	34 C2

ROTHLEY/MOUNTSORREL

Anthony St	34 C6	Marl Fields	34 D3
Arundel Clo	34 A4	Marsh Rd	34 C3
Ash Gro	34 C3	Martin Av	34 B3
Babington Ct	34 C6	Meadow Rd	34 C4
Babington Rd	34 C5	Mere Clo	34 C4
Badgers Bank	34 C5	Montsoreau Way	34 B4
Balmoral Rd	34 B3	Mountsorrel La,	
Barley Way	34 B3	Mountsorrel	34 C3
Barnard Way	34 B3	Mountsorrel La,	
Barons Way	34 C2	South End	34 D1
Beaumaris Rd	34 B4	Mountsorrell and	
Beeches Av	34 C2	Rothley By-Pass	34 C1
Belvoir Clo	34 B4	North St	34 C6
Berkeley Clo	34 C3	Oldfield La	34 C4
Blair Clo	34 B4	Orchard View	34 C4
Bond La	34 A2	Otter La	34 C2
Boundary Rd	34 B3	Paddock Clo	34 C6
Bradgate Clo	34 B1	Partridge Clo	34 D2
Braemar Clo	34 B4	Peppers Clo	34 B1
Breech Hedge	34 C5	Plain Gate	34 A4
Brookland Way	34 A4	Plough Clo	34 B4
Brownhill Cres	34 A6	Pott Acre	34 D3
Bulrush Clo	34 D3	Renning End	34 C4
Caenarvon Clo	34 B4	Rochester Clo	34 B4
Carisbrooke Rd	34 B3	Rockhill Dri	34 B3
Castle Rd	34 B3	Rockingham Rd	34 B4
Cedar Gro	34 C3	Rosslyn Av	34 A3
Celandine Clo	34 D2	Rothley Rd	34 C2
Church Hill Rd	34 B3	Row Leyes Furlong	34 D3
Church St	34 C6	Rowena Ct	34 C4
Cloud Lea	34 C4	Rubicon Clo	34 C3
Clover La	34 D3	Rushey La	34 A2
Conway Rd	34 B3	School St	34 C6
Cossington La	34 D6	Sheepcote	34 C5
Cromwell Rd	34 B4	Sileby Rd	34 C1
Cross Green	34 C5	Skylark Av	34 C3
Cross Hedge	34 C5	Slash La	34 D1
Cross La	34 C4	Speedwell Rd	34 C2
Crown La	34 B2	Stirling Clo	34 A4
Curlew Clo	34 B1	Strachan Clo	34 C3
Danvers Rd	34 C3	Swallow Clo	34 D2
Dover Clo	34 B3	Swan Clo	34 C2
Dunster Rd	34 B3	Swithland La	34 A3
Edinburgh Way	34 B3	Templar Way	34 C5
Elm Clo	34 C3	The Green	34 C2
Fair Mead	34 C4	The Homestead	34 C2
Farnham Clo	34 C5	The Osiers	34 A3
Field Crest	34 B4	The Ridgeway	34 A6
Flaxland	34 C5	The Ridings	34 A4
Forge End	34 C6	The Rise	34 D5
Fort Rd	34 B3	The Romans	34 C3
Fowke St	34 C5	The Roods	34 C5
Furrow Clo	34 C5	Town Green St	34 C6
Garland	34 C5	Walkers La	34 C6
Gipsy La	34 A4	Walton Way	34 B4
Glamis Clo	34 B4	Watling St	34 C2
Glebe Clo	34 B3	Waughs Dri	34 B4
Glenfrith Clo	34 C3	Wellsic La	34 C6
*Glenfrith Gdns,		West Cross La	34 A5
Glenfrith Clo	34 C3	Westfield La	34 A6
Grange La	34 B4	Whatton Oaks	34 C3
Grangefields Dri	34 D5	Willow Gro	34 A3
Granite Way	34 A1	Windmill Clo	34 C2
Greenway Clo	34 C5	Windmill End	34 C5
Hallfields La	34 C6	Windsor Clo	34 B3
		Wood La	34 A1
		Woodfield Rd	34 C5
		Woodgate	34 C6

York Clo	34 B4	Moorfield Pl	35 C3

SHEPSHED

		Morley La	35 B6
Anson Rd	35 A3	Moscow La	35 A6
Arbury Dale	35 D4	Nelson Clo	35 D3
Arundel Gro	35 A5	Neville Clo	35 B3
Ashby Rd Central	35 B5	New Walk	35 B2
Ashby Rd East	35 D5	Newark Clo	35 A4
Ashby Rd West	35 A5	Newlands Av	35 C5
Balmoral Av	35 B4	Nook Clo	35 C1
Banbury Dri	35 A4	Northwood Dri	35 C1
Beaumaris Cres	35 A4	Norwich Clo	35 A4
Belton St	35 B2	Nursery Clo	35 C1
Belvoir Way	35 A4	Oakley Av	35 B2
Beresford Ct	35 C3	Oakley Clo	35 C2
Black Brook	35 A4	Oakley Rd	35 B2
Blacksmiths Av	35 D2	Old Station Clo	35 B5
Boundary Way	35 D1	Oxford St	35 B4
Brendon Clo	35 D5	Oxley Clo	35 B4
Brick Kiln La	35 A6	Park Av	35 C5
Bridge St	35 C2	Park Clo	35 B3
Britannia St	35 C3	Park Rise	35 B3
Brook St	35 C2	Patterson Pl	35 C2
Brookside Clo	35 C4	Pear Tree Av	35 D3
Butthole La	35 C2	Penine Clo	35 D5
Caernarfon Clo	35 B4	Penrith Av	35 A4
Caistor Croft	35 A4	Pentland Av	35 D4
Cambridge St	35 C5	Pick St	35 B2
Carr La	35 A1	Piper Clo	35 C1
Central Av	35 C4	Ploughmans Dri	35 C2
Challotte	35 C3	Polden Clo	35 D5
Chapel St	35 C2	Porlock Clo	35 D4
Charnwood Rd	35 B5	Pudding Bag La	35 A6
Chatsworth Clo	35 A3	Purbeck Av	35 D4
Chestnut Clo	35 D3	Purley Clo	35 D4
Cheviot Dri	35 D4	Quantock Rise	35 D4
Chiltern Av	35 D3	Queen St	35 C3
Church Gate	35 C3	Radnor Dri	35 C1
Church Side	35 C3	Ring Fence	35 B4
Church St	35 C2	Ringwood Rd	35 C1
Coach Rd	35 D3	Rockingham Clo	35 A5
Coachmans Ct	35 D2	Romway Clo	35 C4
Conway Dri	35 A4	St Bernards Clo	35 B4
Coombe Clo	35 C5	St Botolph Rd	35 C4
Cotton Croft	35 C4	St James Rd	35 C4
Countrymans Way	35 C3	St Winifride Rd	35 C4
Cumbrian Way	35 D3	*Salmon Mews,	
Danvers La	35 C3	Britannia St	35 C3
Deacon Clo	35 C3	Sandringham Rise	35 A4
Domont Clo	35 B4	Shepherds Clo	35 C2
Dovecote	35 C2	Smithy Way	35 D3
Factory St	35 B2	Snowden Clo	35 D5
Fairway Rd	35 C3	Spring Clo	35 C5
Fairway Rd Sth	35 C5	Spring La	35 C5
Field Av	35 C1	Springfield Rd	35 B4
Field St	35 C3	Sullington Rd	35 C4
Forest St	35 C3	Tamworth Clo	35 A4
Forman Rd	35 C4	Temple Clo	35 D5
Freehold St	35 C3	Tetbury Dri	35 A4
Garendon Clo	35 C3	The Inleys	35 D3
Garendon Rd	35 C3	The Lant	35 B4
Gelders Hall Rd	35 B5	The Meadows	35 B4
Glenfields	35 B3	Thorpe Rd	35 B4
Glenmore Clo	35 B3	Tickow La	35 A3
Grange La	35 B3	Trueway Dri	35 D4
Grange Rd	35 A3	Trueway Dri Sth	35 D4
Griffin Clo	35 A4	Tyler Ct	35 C1
Hall Croft	35 C3	Wellyard Clo	35 D3
Hallamford Rd	35 A1	Westoby Clo	35 D3
Harrington Rd	35 D3	Wicklow Clo	35 D4
Hathern Rd	35 D1	Wightman Clo	35 C3
Highfields Clo	35 C1	Windsor Dri	35 B4
Holt Rise	35 C5	Wood Clo	35 D3
Homeway Clo	35 D4	Woodlands Dri	35 C1
Ingleberry Rd	35 C6	Woodmans Way	35 C1
Iveshead Rd	35 B6	Wortley Clo	35 D1
Jolly Farmers La	35 B6		

SILEBY/RATCLIFFE ON THE WREAKE

Jubilee Path	35 A5		
Kings Rd	35 B5	Ainsworth Dri	38 C2
Kirkhill	35 C3	Albert Av	38 B2
Lacey Ct	35 C3	Albion Rd	38 A3
Lambert Av	35 B3	Avenue Rd	38 B3
Lansdowne Av	35 C1	Back La	38 A3
Lansdowne Rd	35 C1	Barnards Dri	38 C2
Leicester Rd	35 C4	Barradale Av	38 A2
Lindley Av	35 C4	Barrow Rd	38 A2
Little Haw La	35 A3	Blackberry La	38 C4
Longcliffe Rd	35 A4	Bowling Green Clo	38 B2
Loughborough Rd	35 C2	Brook St	38 A3
Ludlow Pl	35 A4	Broome La	38 E4
Malvern Av	35 C4	Brushfield Av	38 C2
Manor Gdns	35 B2	Cauby Clo	38 C2
Market Pl	35 B3	Cemetery Rd	38 B3
McCarthy Rd	35 B3	Chalfont Dri	38 A4
Mendip Clo	35 D1	Charles St	38 A4
Mill Clo	35 D1	Church La, Ratcliffe	38 F4

Church La, Sileby	38 A
Claire Ct	38 C
Collingwood Dri	38 B
Cossington La	38 A
Dickens Clo	38 B
East Orchard	38 A
Finsbury Av	38 C
Flaxland Cres	38 A
Forest Dri	38 A
Fosse Way	38 B
Gibson Rd	38 B
Greedon Rise	38 A
Hanover Dri	38 B
Haybrook Rd	38 B
Heathcote Dri	38 B
Hickling Dri	38 B
High St	38 A
Highbridge	38 A
Highgate Rd	38 B
Hobbswick	38 B
Homefield Rd	38 B
Hudson Rd	38 A
Humble La	38 D
INDUSTRIAL ESTATES:	
Albion Rd Ind Est	38 B
Jubilee Av	38 B
Kendal Rd	38 B
Kilbourne Clo	38 B
King St	38 A
Lanes Clo	38 B
Main St	38 F
Manor Dri	38 A
Marshall Av	38 A
Middle Orchard	38 A
Milner Clo	38 A
Molyneux Dri	38 B
Moreton Dale	38 B
Mountsorrel La	38 A
Newbold Cl	38 B
North Hill Clo	38 C
Park Rd	38 A
Parsons Dri	38 C
Peashill Clo	38 C
Phoenix Dri	38 B
Pryor Rd	38 B
Quaker Rd	38 A
Ratcliffe Rd	38 B
St Gregorys Dri	38 B
St Marys Rd	38 A
Seagrave Rd	38 A
Sherrards Dri	38 A
Springfield Rd	38 B
Stanage Rd	38 C
Staveley Clo	38 B
Storer Clo	38 B
Swan St	38 A
The Banks	38 A
Wallace Dri	38 B
Wards Cres	38 B
Weldon Av	38 B
Wellbrook Av	38 B

SYSTON/EAST GOSCOTE

Abbots Clo	36 D
Albert St	37 E
*Albion Par,	
Albion St	37 E
Albion St	37 E
Anthony Clo	36 C
Archdale St	36 C
Archers Grn	37 F
Ash Dri	37 E
Augustus Clo	36 C
Avenue Rd	37 G
Avery Dri	37 E
Back La	36 E
Badgers Cnr	37 G
Badminton Rd	37 E
Balliol Av	37 F
Barkby La	36 C
Barkby Rd	37 E
Barry Dri	37 E
Bath St	37 E
Beatty Rd	37 F
Beeby Clo	37 F
Beech Rd	37 E
Beechwood Av	37 G
Belvoir Dri	37 F
Bennetts La	36 E
Blackberry La	36 B
Blackthorn Dri	36 C
Bluebell Clo	37 G
Bracken Dale	37 G
Brighton Av	37 F
Broad St	37 E